WORLD ARMAMENT AND WORLD HUNGER

Willy Brandt, born in 1913, fled Germany in 1933 and lived in exile in Norway and Sweden during the Second World War. Having joined Germany's Social Democratic Party (SPD) in 1931, he entered politics after his return home in 1945. He was Governing Mayor of West Berlin from 1957 to 1966, in which year he became Vice Chancellor and Foreign Minister in the CDU/SPD Coalition. From 1969–1974 he was German Chancellor in the SPD/FDP Government.

He has been President of the Socialist International since 1976 and, from 1979–1983, a member of the European Parliament. In 1971 Willy Brandt won the Nobel Prize for Peace.

He is the author of many books and essays and the Independent Commission on International Development Issues, which he chaired, produced two reports —*North–South: A Programme for Survival* (1980) and *Common Crisis: North–South: Cooperation for World Recovery* (1983). Willy Brandt has been Chairman of the SPD since 1964.

WORLD ARMAMENT AND WORLD HUNGER

A Call for Action

WILLY BRANDT

Translated by Anthea Bell

LONDON
VICTOR GOLLANCZ LTD
1986

First published in West Germany in October 1985
as *Der organisierte Wahnsinn*

First published in Great Britain 1986
by Victor Gollancz Ltd,
14 Henrietta Street, London WC2E 8QJ

© 1985 by Verlag Kiepenheuer & Witsch, Köln
Translation © Victor Gollancz Ltd 1986

British Library Cataloguing in Publication Data
Brandt, Willy
    World armament and world hunger: a call for action.
    1. Economic policy   2. Economic development
    I. Title   II. Der organisierte Wahnsinn. *English*
    330.9   HD82

    ISBN 0-575-03826-8
    ISBN 0-575-03827-6 Pbk

Photoset in Great Britain by
Rowland Phototypesetting Ltd,
Bury St Edmunds, Suffolk
and printed by Billing & Sons Ltd, Worcester

CONTENTS

FOREWORD

Why this book? I have often been asked what became of the recommendations of the Independent Commission on International Development Issues which I chaired. I have tried to give an honest answer; I cannot give a very positive one.

Over the last few years some progress has been made in some developing countries, but much further deterioration has also occurred, as is shown by both the famine disaster in Africa and the debt crisis in Latin America. This survey, however, which is not written for experts, does not suggest we resign ourselves. Instead, it calls for productive concern.

It is against our own interests to leave the developing countries to deal with their economic and social problems alone, instead of recognizing them as our partners. World peace is at risk if the East–West conflict and the arms race spread ever further into the Third World — and if funds are not at long last released from the build-up of armaments and made available for the struggle against underdevelopment.

I would therefore draw attention to the connections between East–West and North–South relations, between the arms race and world hunger.

I should like to thank Gerhard Thiebach for his work on the material, Fritz Fischer for helpful comments, and my wife for going through the manuscript.

Unkel, Spring 1985   W.B.

INTRODUCTION TO THE BRITISH EDITION

We live in times full of drama and confusion. What we are experiencing is not a process of measurable change, but a series of wide-ranging upheavals in science and technology, in economic affairs and in international relations.

Numerous crises in many parts of the world provide ample evidence of this radical change. But it would be quite wrong to allow ourselves to be hypnotized by that suggestive term 'crisis'. There is no hope of things simply returning to normal. We will continue to face radical change and we must find adequate solutions. Not to do so could be fatal.

To my way of thinking, worldwide change is necessary today for three main reasons. First, there is the need for a profound restructuring of the world economy to increase world productivity and to provide jobs. Secondly, there is the persistent East–West rivalry and arms build-up. And last, but not least, are the completely unsatisfactory North–South relations between the industrialized states on the one hand and the developing countries on the other.

First, the profound change in the pattern of the world's economy: The period of persistent economic growth on the scale which we experienced in the Fifties and Sixties would seem to be over for the foreseeable future. This holds true for the whole world. In western industrialized countries, in the eastern industrial societies and in the developing countries as a group – wherever we look there is now much slower economic progress. In some parts we even see output declining.

We do not need to look far for the social and political consequences. For many years, it was possible to offset social tensions in western democratic societies because there was enough economic growth to go around for all, or almost all. As a result, even the broad masses of our nations derived benefit from a steadily rising level of affluence. Whenever divergent interests met head-on, a material compromise was at hand.

Today, this sort of compromise is available only on a rather limited scale. In many countries, the pace of social strife has quickened, even if everyone may not yet be aware of it.

It will require a considerable amount of imagination and sensitivity to balance the various interests in our modern industrial societies within the limits to further growth which are now visible, and at the same time to maintain a smoothly functioning political process. Our democracies will not remain what they have been if our elected leaders leave the field uncontested to rival groups or simply stand aside.

If a new balance among the various factions and interests is not achieved, there will be an acceleration of a trend already noticeable in certain places: a loss of confidence in those in political office along with a dwindling faith in the viability of modern democracy. I see the possibility of an ever more widespread alienation – alienation of the sort expressed by quite a number of the younger people – an escapism inspired by a blend of political weariness and anxiety about modern civilization. Misgivings about the whole purpose of technical progress might combine with a dangerous nostalgia for the apparent peacefulness and tranquillity of former times – a peacefulness and tranquillity which never really existed.

Secondly: The arms race has not only continued apace, it has assumed dimensions which can no longer be grasped by the human mind. Every day the world spends millions and millions of dollars for military purposes; we stockpile more explosives than food, and we are more concerned with what is called military security than with hunger and malnutrition, which in the end may pose an even greater threat. Every warning seems to have fallen on deaf ears. All efforts to achieve concrete arms limitation seemed to be frustrated by the feeling of a growing threat from the other side. Sometimes, warnings miscarry because the overall situation becomes unstable. And regional conflicts expand. It is small wonder that many people were beginning to ask whether the policy of détente ever really existed, and if it did whether or not it had failed definitely, and if it had what alternative there might be.

It is still my feeling that the ideas underlying the efforts to reduce tension at the end of the Sixties and the beginning of the Seventies have not been futile. In my view, these ideas did not flow from illusions, but from the pragmatic desire to supplement defence with a political dimension for safeguarding peace, producing attempts to help evolve a common interest in arms limitation. That remains indispensable. And it has, as we know, led to reopening of talks between the two superpowers.

The further commitment of valuable resources to even more gigantic arms projects would render it impossible to devote one's attention to the great problems which exist side by side with the arms race, with equally frightening possibilities. And we may well fool ourselves when we see security as purely a military problem, as if population explosion and hunger, the limited resource base of our earth and the abuse of the environment were risks of a lesser category.

Still, we must not become discouraged. However painful setbacks may be, they don't give us an excuse for simply turning our backs. The important thing is to learn from mankind's mistakes and to stay on course for peace and cooperation: without illusions, but with steadfastness.

Thirdly: Reshaping relations between industrialized and developing countries – 'North and South', as it is often called in international discussions. In point of fact, this much used term 'North–South' inadequately conveys the complexity of highly different levels of development and gravely imbalanced relations between rich and poor peoples, richer and poorer nations. But it is certainly no exaggeration when I say that I regard this as *the* social challenge of our times – a challenge to all people with a sense of responsibility.

Today, one-fifth of humanity suffers from hunger and malnutrition in developing countries. The majority of these men, women and children live in South and South-East Asia and the sub-Saharan regions of Africa. During the last decade, many countries in these regions have been able to make but little progress. If no fundamental changes take place, then this decade cannot be expected to bring any improvements either. It might well mean more *under*development.

Therefore, it is perfectly understandable that the developing nations have been calling for fundamental reforms in the world economy for something like two decades. However, as in the case of domestic reforms in most of our own countries, the scope for international reforms has narrowed considerably.

The picture I have just drawn is not a very happy one, but it does reflect the real situation. Under these circumstances, we must try to implement adequate policies. It seems clear to me that employment policy and structural policy accompanying it cannot be left solely to the oft-invoked 'self-healing forces' of the market economy. Anyone who has held a position of responsibility in a country like mine in recent years will never be tempted to underestimate the thrust of the market-economy system. Nevertheless, experience at home and abroad, especially in less developed countries, leads me to believe that an important role must be played by public responsibility in a number of sectors.

At the same time, everyone with a knowledge of the current situation in the public sector, and in large private enterprise as well, will realize the importance of avoiding bureaucratic excesses. In any case, gross materialism cannot be the sole *raison d'état* in a democracy. I am not pleading the virtues of high-minded renunciation; I am pleading the case of justice, solidarity and fair treatment, both within states and between states. In a period of rapid and deep-rooted change, we shall only survive if individual interests are embedded within an overall framework of social solidarity. From this flows the perception that government decisions must be taken with the closest possible involvement of the people concerned and affected by such measures.

The holders of political office must remain receptive to fresh ideas, whether they themselves are able to develop them or not. Those who believe that many things cannot continue as they have in the past must be taken seriously. Should we not be mounting a more active search for solutions which correspond to the economic and ecological requirements of our time in order to establish, wherever possible, a stable equilibrium?

So what is the plan of action? First and most important, the leaders of the two superpowers must discharge their specific responsibilities towards other nations. They must do what has to be done in order to create that minimum of confidence without which predictability is impossible. Otherwise, there will be no end to the arms race, and without an end to the arms race, détente cannot survive; and without détente there can be only a fragile security.

Europe has long ceased to be the hub of the world. Nevertheless, it remains of great importance for the whole of mankind that we in Europe prove capable of maintaining peace and thereby furnish an example of how differing interests can be reconciled without explosive conflicts. It is my firm belief that we need détente in order to safeguard peace and to find the strength for balancing the interests of North and South.

My conclusion derives from lifelong experience – a life marked by ups and downs, disappointments and encouragements. What humanity needs is not less détente, but more negotiations and cooperation. In addition to humanitarian and idealistic challenges, there is a good deal of legitimate self-interest involved. Peace is not only good for others. More exchange will be to our advantage as well as to that of others. The jobs of many of our young people, and even more so, of their children, will depend upon speeding up the process of development and exchange.

It will be difficult for anyone to escape the conclusion, after reading this book, that interdependence is the dominant fact of life in our era – that we are responsible for each other's well-being, and that we must learn to live together or face the prospect of perishing together.

I am not without hope. Indeed, realistic confidence in our capacity to build a better world for all has been the foundation of my thinking and the motivation of my work.

All of us are responsible for helping to create our common future.

Bonn, Spring 1986   W.B.

I

A QUESTION OF COMMON SURVIVAL

1. *Appalling Discrepancies*

Most of us have no idea of the alarming record 1986 will leave behind: very probably in that one year over 1,000 billion dollars will have been spent, worldwide, on military purposes of various kinds.

Look at this vast expenditure of funds in another way: every minute of every day of the week – work days and holidays alike – the nations of the world are spending around two million dollars on armaments and other military expenditure.

And every minute, some 30 children aged under five or six are dying because they do not have enough to eat, or there is no clean water for them, and because they are denied any kind of medical care.

In 1974, an admirable pronouncement was made: within a decade no child should go to bed hungry. This was directly after the Sahel zone and Bangladesh famine disasters of that time. In 1984 UNICEF, the United Nations Children's Fund, calculated that 40,000 children in the age group mentioned were dying every day.

The shocking television pictures of the latest East African disasters have roused many from apathy, although the pictures convey only a part of the terrible truth. For experts tell us that the world is now producing, and has at its disposal, enough food to feed the whole of humanity.

I believe that even if there were no other discrepancy to challenge our common sense of human responsibility than this – that millions of children starve to death when they could be saved with a fraction of the funds spent on the build-up of armaments – it ought to move us to anger. Nor should we allow ourselves to be fobbed off with nonsense couched in political leaders' jargon.

However, the number of those who recognize the existence and the glaring injustice of this discrepancy is growing, though such people may express what they feel in very different ways, because of their different cultures and political systems. Avoidable hunger *is* a glaring injustice, on a large scale. And systems, whether national or international, are to blame if they cannot overcome glaring injustice and avert great danger for mankind. There are many, particularly young people, who feel deep distress when confronted by persistent hunger among vast numbers of individuals over large areas of the world, when it could be relieved with a small part of the funds absorbed by ever-increasing military expenditure. (It makes no difference to this argument whether estimated expenditure on armaments is set slightly too high or actually lags behind the reality.)

A few years ago, an Asian friend of mine, now dead, put the question of priorities in his own way: why had President Kennedy appealed to his country's scientists not to be content simply to take up the challenge of the Soviet Sputnik (of which they had scientific understanding at the time)? Why had Kennedy set them the task of putting an American on the moon? And why had the scientists asked for ten years to do it and 20 billion dollars? My Nepalese friend, B. P. Koirala, who was even better acquainted with his country's prisons than with its seat of government, and who asked his questions quietly, having cancer of the larynx, but no less forcibly for that, wondered why fifty billion could not be mobilized to help conquer the worst of global poverty.

We are not concerned with details here, but with the basic principle, which is absolutely sound. Equally sound is the method of putting it into practice: initially by reallocating 10 or even just 5 per cent of global armaments expenditure, at the same time making it clear that this would be in the interests of the richer countries and the more prosperous sections of humanity themselves, and showing just how much that would be the case. But obviously many of those in power in the East and the West, the North and the South still (and for how much longer?) regard it as wrong to reduce arms expenditure by a modest percentage, and, instead, using the funds for productive purposes. Using them, indeed, to finance projects which would accord as much with the precepts of solidarity and love for one's neighbour, as with the well-understood self-interest of those states which would be most affected by this modest reallocation of resources – including, in the long term, the interests of their security.

It is now being said by eminent if not altogether conservative experts that the only way to overcome the international financial crisis will be to divert funds earmarked for defence budgets. Over the last few years I have said repeatedly (and I have not let the mockery of officialdom deter me) that the unrestrained squandering of funds on arms policies has contributed very largely to the current difficulties of the international economy. To put it even more bluntly: the arms race inhibits the development of the world economy.

Not only the economic consequences, however, but other connections in this context have long gone unrecognized. I remember a discussion in Berlin in the early summer of 1978, to which I was invited by the Aspen Institute. I spoke on the connections between arms and development, an unfamiliar train of thought to most of my otherwise knowledgeable audience, and I had no cause to complain of any inattention. Then, however, one participant of whom I thought particularly highly came out with his opinion that arms control was so difficult a subject, I would do better not to make it even more complicated by mixing it up with 'issues of development aid' . . . I have not been able to take that advice.

The tendency to keep East–West and North–South issues scrupulously apart – except in 'strategic' questions – has now slightly lessened. Reference to the way North–South relations have acquired a new dimension in the struggle for world peace is no longer contradicted with quite such a lack of understanding. And more people acknowledge that mass misery and extreme underdevelopment have become *the* great social challenge of our time. Such understanding alone does not, of course, get us very far. But in order to act judiciously we must realize some simple truths.

Where mass hunger reigns, we cannot speak of peace. If we want to get rid of war, we must ban mass misery too. Morally, it makes no difference whether human beings are killed in war or condemned to death by starvation. The international community – in the dual sense of concerned citizens and responsible governments – has no more important task, besides controlling the build-up of arms, than overcoming mass hunger and other sources of misery which could be avoided.

We must not let ourselves be blinded or paralysed by the gigantic, scarcely conceivable size of the figures involved. Nor is the moral challenge to our common humanity to be assessed by calculating whether the sum of human misery is even greater than the given estimates, or perhaps a little less, but solely by the possibility of feeding our hungry fellow men and women. We must come to realize that a sense of solidarity with those who are so much worse off is also the way to find partners in a world that needs cooperation; this is true not least of the economy.

Vast rounded-up numbers can easily make the fate of individuals involved congeal into statistics. Astronomical figures overtax our capacity to grasp them. I remember how during the Second World War under Nazi tyranny, a sense of the sheer extent of the toll being taken – the numbers of the fallen, murdered, imprisoned, exiled – was in great danger of being lost, or never even felt at all. Churchill once said that if a human being dies, it is a tragedy; if 100,000 die, it is statistics. We can identify more easily with a small number, particularly in a familiar environment. Victims on a scale of millions become an abstract idea, with no sense of closeness to it. One nought more or less conveys little to us.

But there is no help for it: we must familiarize ourselves with the reality behind those huge figures. We must try to make the meaning they obscure clear to ourselves (and others): 450 to 500 million people, at a cautious estimate, are undernourished or suffer chronic hunger. It is small comfort to know that the figure was even higher five years ago; in the report published early in 1980 by the Commission I chaired, the number of those suffering from malnutrition was put at 500 to 600 million. The impression of obscene horror is further reinforced by the fact that no institute – or governmental department, or international organization – is in a position to make calculations which are anywhere near exact and which agree. Often they disagree over the extent of the

arbitrarily drawn by foreign masters) for their economic de-colonization – or simply their ability to survive.

- The population of the world has doubled to 4.8 billion.
- Gross world product as statistically recorded (that is, the sum of goods and services produced in the world's states or national economies) has quadrupled; so has energy consumption.
- There is still a gulf between rich and poor, and in some ways it is even wider, but the dividing line does not coincide with the division between developing and industrial countries: there is depressing poverty to be found in the North, and equally there is provocative superfluity in the South.
- Great achievements in science and technology must be set against a good deal on the debit side: natural resources are being plundered, and the process reveals the lack of restraint in an economy over-orientated towards a narrow concept of its own profitable interests – or towards bureaucratically planned targets which are remote from reality.
- The use of nuclear energy has become reality, but has not had the expected results: the problems of defusing anxiety about it have not been solved. Its military use could cause untold harm if theories of deterrence, or the nerves of those concerned, or computer reliability should fail.
- After an unmanned (Soviet) satellite began circling the earth in 1959, and a manned (American) module landed on the moon in 1969 – you will recall my Nepalese friend's question in connection with those events – a man-made device left the solar system for the first time in 1983. The militarization of space is now in progress, and has caused additional insecurity.
- While the East–West conflict and North–South problems mingle, the arms race between the superpowers has spread to large areas of the world, originally unaffected, where it has found company and been imitated.
- Despite all our progress in science and technology, in the dissemination and sharing of knowledge, the states of the world have not mastered their political, economic and indeed ecological difficulties, individually or as a body. Whether the point at issue is the arms race or world hunger, the environment or energy, unemployment or inadequate social welfare, we meet everywhere with irrational procedures.

My first thesis, nevertheless, is that in the medium and long term, North and South have more interests in common or running parallel – and so do East and West, particularly here in Europe – than most people have yet recognized. This should not be confused with having an eye to short-term economic advantage.

My other thesis is that a faster tempo of development in the South will also benefit people in the North. This proposition has been much criticized for being allegedly based on a 'Keynesian' concept, an objection which, however, has nothing to do with economic theory, but is part of an attempt to talk urgent problems out of existence and defend a form of international relations in which the weaker goes to the wall. Lord Keynes' theories aside, the regions of the world cannot afford an international economic policy of a self-centred and keenly competitive nature for very much longer. Global dangers are growing, and it is highly inadvisable to leave them out of our economic calculations.

In any case, the industrial countries clearly have an interest, one that needs no kind of interpretation in terms of economic theory, in strengthening their economic and in particular their agricultural involvement with other parts of the world. Any calculation, even one of only medium-term relevance, will lead to that conclusion.

Among circumstances that have changed is the fact that what was previously described as the 'world economy' has now, for the first time in history, actually become 'global', if not yet as unambiguously so as has technology. But while we can observe a process of internationalization in the economic area, many states are still excluded from decision-making. We also have the peculiarities of the system. Matters of international economic importance are still decided by those states which hold economic and financial power. Even in the European Community, we perpetuate the anachronism of making 'national' decisions on matters which can no longer be decided at national level.

How far can the uncertainties of the international economy since the early Seventies be attributed to the poor development of North–South relations? Can one deny that the oil price crisis had far-reaching effects, not least on the economic activities of those developing countries which are not oil producers? Is there any doubt that the rise in exports from the newly industrialized developing countries has created problems in many markets? And, can one seek the source of the worldwide economic failures of the last ten or fifteen years – with regard to monetary stability, growth, employment, international trade – anywhere but in the centres whence the great crisis of the Thirties itself proceeded?

As one who saw where it led last time, I ask: who can really tell whether the crisis of the Eighties will be overcome any better than the crisis of the Thirties? There are more than 30 million unemployed in Western industrial countries: that is no light matter. The figures in which absolute poverty is expressed can only horrify a normal mind. Reference to the depth of the structural change can at least convey something of the gravity of the problems we have to surmount. But one cannot see how the connections between issues of finance, trade, commodities and food are to be controlled.

The economic situation certainly appeared rather better in 1984–5 than a few years earlier; there was a remarkable upswing in the USA, and also in Canada and Japan, less so in Europe. There was no all-clear for the poorer countries; many of them experienced stagnation and retrogression. And there was widespread speculation as to when we might expect the next American recession. Meanwhile, the extent to which the United States was financing its budget deficits by 'blood transfusions' was something to be viewed with concern, as was the unfortunate effect of the high interest rates associated with them. (In the early summer of 1984, one of the big banks of the USA was barely saved from collapse.) World trade and economic activity, said one of the International Monetary Fund's forecasts, which are usually not so bad, would perceptibly lose impetus in 1985–6. For the rest, I can only suggest from my own experience that we should not let prophets bluff us over the international economy.

When my Commission published its Report six years ago, we thought it imperative for governments to apply themselves, urgently, to the issue of North–South cooperation and give it a more constructive form. Otherwise, we feared, the international situation would deteriorate even further. And we were right: the situation has indeed deteriorated. I am not suggesting that we should now resign ourselves to despair on that account. But why

A growing number of people will stand by these simple truths:

- That a precipitate increase in global expenditure on armaments is almost inevitably accompanied by economic setbacks and social damage – even if the great powers may sometimes manage to hang their own millstones around other necks.
- That the international monetary system has come adrift because it was not well enough adapted to fundamental change in the structure of the system of states.
- That even in the industrial countries, more employment could be created if we could at last manage to create the financial prerequisites for bringing together the unsupplied needs of the 'South' with our own surplus capacities.
- That it must impose intolerable burdens even on the industrial countries if the revenues of the developing countries from their commodity exports are reduced, as they often are, to a fraction of their proper value, while little consideration is given to anticipating the demand for commodities and energy in the years to come.
- That the debt problem – the position at the end of 1984 was that the developing countries were indebted to the amount of at least $850 billion – is due not only to the supposedly irresponsible governments of the debtor countries, but at least as much to their partners bearing responsibility in the creditor nations.

hide the fact that the dangers, taken as a whole, have grown even greater?

3. *Comprehensive Answers to Global Problems*

I cannot over-emphasize: if we neglect the tasks of the present and fail to invest in the future, we may arm ourselves to death without actually waging a major war, and bring our economies to the point of collapse. The North itself can survive only if the South is allowed independence and a decent life.

In 1984, a good deal was written on population questions; the second United Nations conference on population policy took place in Mexico City. In the field of North–South relations, only the Latin American debt mountain and the new famine disaster in Africa aroused anything like comparable interest at the time. Yet almost all that was said at that conference in Mexico had been known for years, and some of us had come to an agreement on it long before. We knew that:

- World population increases by over a million every five days.
- World population will rise from 4.8 billion in 1984 to 6.1 billion at the turn of the century: which means that in the Eighties and Nineties alone, i.e. within two decades, the human race will have increased by almost 2 billion. When I went to school in the year 1920, that was the number of people then living on the earth.
- Nine-tenths of the increase is in Third World countries, which have a very young age structure.

Thus, to a considerable extent, the future is programmed. However, it still remains to be seen whether world population can be stabilized at ten or twelve billion in the middle of the next century. I write this as one who has learned that this is another area in which excessive agitation is out of place. From all we now know, the earth has room for more people than was thought in my youth, and even later.

But world population cannot expand indefinitely, and faster than economic output. It is up to our human will and not Fate to decide whether the population explosion, as it is frequently called, actually ends in destruction or not.

Twenty years ago one aroused smiles, or outright laughter, by merely hinting at the consequences the ruthless plundering of the earth would have for future generations. Many people are now becoming aware of the dangers, and the measures we have failed to take. First the warnings of the Club of Rome, then the American *Global 2000* report, presented to President Carter in 1980, made it clear that protection of the environment is a genuinely global issue: there is *world*wide air pollution, there are serious *world*wide threats to our water and our forests; species of

25

plants and animals are disappearing in great numbers and within a short period of time. Retribution is coming for the thoughtless and narrow perception of economic interests, and only a few people realize that there are limits to the exploitation of nature.

What it will mean if trees are no longer able to counteract the pollution of the air is slowly dawning. But can our imaginative faculties gauge the climatic consequences of the disappearance of the Amazonian forests? Many people on our earth are busily engaged in turning the dreadful vision of a global environmental catastrophe into reality.

In addition, an ever closer connection emerges not just between hunger and armaments, but between the environment and security. Here, even more than elsewhere, we see that the *status quo* must not be confused with stability.

Are we really going to put our faith in what is ideologically seen as the free play of supposedly free forces to save what may yet be saved? Or are we going to address ourselves to problems which can be resolved only by mutually coordinated action? It ought not to be hard to answer that question once we have even an inkling of, for instance, the effect of continued deforestation. I am not and never was in favour of playing off North–South and environmental issues against each other. When I received the Nobel Peace Prize, I spoke on both those aspects of our global domestic policy, and added, 'If the natural supplies of water, oxygen and living matter on our planet run out, then humanity, poisoned and starving, will no longer care about the peaceful order for which we strive today.'

Since then, argument has been piled upon argument in emphatic refutation of those arrogant folk who think they know everything, and do not; managers of the 'established disorder' who like to be acclaimed as practical politicians, but really thrive only because ordinary citizens do not see through (or want to see through) their complacent trickery. Human reaction certainly falls far short of what it should be to the consequences of the changes I have outlined. But a sense is spreading that we are dealing with problems that are more and more significant to the *whole* world. The worldwide interdependence of problems is a sign of the times in which we live.

And there is an increasing concentration of problems which

exist independently of a country's political and social systems and alignment within world politics. Whether research is done at institutes in Boston or Moscow, whether critical minds are debating and analysing problems in São Paulo or Bombay, Peking or Tokyo, Berlin or Paris, men and women everywhere are recognizing that not only they themselves, their country or their people are affected; the great questions of the future concern humanity as a whole.

I am not claiming that community of interests can derive from this except in the recognition of mutual dependency, and perhaps also in a growing understanding of the threats to the survival of mankind (which can only be joint survival). Among enlightened and open-minded people, there can be no doubt that we face the enormous task of ensuring humanity's survival *together*, and can master it only by international cooperation. Neither the rich North nor the poor South – nor the West without, and in opposition to, the East – will be able to control their problems alone and without mutually coordinated action.

We are thus concerned with more than 'aid for the poor' – important as empathy and a sense of joint responsibility for our fellow men are and will remain. We are concerned with a view of the tasks ahead of us in the international economic context. The production of goods and the provision of services are going to be increasingly based on the worldwide division of labour. The market – not automatically the same thing as space for unrestricted trade policies to have free play – for an increasing number of industries will be a worldwide market. International economy will not just be so called, it really will be international – for good or ill.

Potential danger building up in one region – whether in power politics, the economy, the ecology or perhaps in population policy – will no longer leave other regions unaffected in the long term. Ecological and economic interaction, in particular, extend far beyond specific areas. The threat of the consequences of the arms race has long been affecting more people than those immediately involved.

Global and interdependent problems call for comprehensive solutions. By this I do not mean that as many tasks as possible should not be tackled regionally; in many cases this is the only feasible way, particularly if it remains as difficult as ever to safeguard international interests through intergovernmental institutions. But the tackling of tasks on a regional basis will itself prove beneficial only if mutual consideration and the conciliation of interests are observed.

There is hardly a state in the world economically strong enough to do without the conciliation of interests. That also applies to blocs and federations of states. The really important problems are of a character that transcends systems. The political system of a country and the form its economy and society take will certainly influence its ability to solve problems. But many tasks and many dangers dependent on commodities, environmental threats, the results of technological change have to be dealt with wherever industrialization progresses. There will be a race between systems to see how problems can best be resolved. But there will be no more room for one region to pursue a path of its own without coming to an understanding with other parts of the world.

I am well aware that the thesis of *one* world, of the global nature of our problems and the interdependence of the world's various regions is sometimes dismissed as a myth – in the West, in the East, in the developing countries too. I have examined the arguments with the utmost readiness to exercise self-criticism, and I cannot find my thesis disproved. Indeed, many of the objections raised strike me as being marked, rather, by a disinclination to overcome cherished notions, egotism, or simply the defensive pragmatism of the politics of the day.

Over the last few years, we have frequently heard it said that the economic situation of the leading industrial countries must improve before more can be done for the developing countries and for North–South cooperation. I have always taken this for an excuse. For such an attitude fails to recognize the advantages that faster and better development of the Third World can mean for *all* concerned.

It would be presumptuous of me to examine those answers offered to my fellow men and women of widely differing cultures in response to the most profound of all questions. Or to whatever beliefs they hold concerning free will and what is allegedly unalterable. But without touching upon religious or ideological convictions too closely, I would say that not only should serious misgivings be voiced, a sharp protest must be raised if we – which generally means those who govern us – meet humanity's questions about survival with a positive unwillingness to take responsibility.

When the Federal Republic of Germany was still in its infancy, I said to my friends that we could not and did not wish to go without the friendship of the peoples of the former colonies. 'We do not want them as allies in the Cold War, but as friends whom we meet on terms of respect for their own ways, their own traditions, and their particular situations.'

At the time, 25 years ago, most of us did not yet realize that we were in a unique position. In the whole history of humanity, its survival has never before been in question. For in no previous generation have men and women been able to annihilate the species as a whole, whether as the result of a war waged with nuclear weapons; or as the inevitable consequence of continued exploitation of the environment and its natural resources; or the strangulation of national economies as an alternative to investing in the future.

4. *Whose Mutual Interest?*

Confronting and possibly overcoming the North–South conflict is *the* great social challenge of our time. It is worth while looking to see where – despite all the differences in our assumptions, standards, convictions and ideologies – areas of mutual or related interest between the industrial and the developing countries may be found.

I know that this attitude is regarded with considerable distrust in parts of the Third World: are factors that are really incompatible to be lumped together? Or is the idea to explain differences away instead of helping to overcome them? Is it perhaps a fresh attempt at exchanging direct for indirect dependence, promoting imperialism by other means?

To cite one extreme case of polemics: when I was in Latin America in the autumn of 1984, I encountered not only the hackneyed criticism of those who thought I should have expressed myself in friendlier terms where Washington was concerned; I was also harshly criticized by the 'Left'. A hostile Brazilian journalist thought that I had merely intended to 'throw sand in the eyes' of the people of the Third World with my speeches on disarmament and the debt crisis, and the same applied to the report of my Commission; that I was attempting 'to eliminate the class struggle on the international plane' with ideas of peaceful dialogue and cooperation; that I wanted to give a slightly more human face to capitalism, with the real intention of perpetuating it through the exploitation of the peoples of the Third World; and that I imagined 'the proletarian nations' as being 'on their knees, begging bowl in hand, meekly asking for a little improvement in the distribution of international revenues . . .'

It is hard not to return an angry answer, but to what end? Suppose we were all, each in his own sphere of action and influence, to make concrete efforts to identify and repel the enemies of just solutions? There are far too many, even among the rich upper classes of the developing countries, who parrot phrases about the 'class struggle on the international plane', instead of applying themselves to urgently needed reforms in their own lands.

The scepticism that I have in fact often encountered was related in no small degree – even when free of hostility – to the question of whether enlightened self-interest can be an element in the common interest, and to whether those who thought like myself really believed it was possible to do away with the fundamental differences between master and servant, exploiters and exploited. Did we seriously mean to patch matters up where a clean break was called for, to practise appeasement where a struggle was inevitable?

It is sometimes asked, rather sharply, in *whose* mutual interests adaptation or conciliation would actually be, and the suspicion is frequently voiced that people who think as I do may overrate the specific experience of their own countries. Yet was not a long and laborious learning process necessary before we ourselves came to realize that higher pay increased mass buying power and was a considerable spur to our domestic economies? Greater social justice is an incitement to economic development. Can conclusions of benefit to the world economy be drawn from that?

I do *not* mean that we want to make our own model a universal criterion, or assume that our own variety of capitalist development should be set up elsewhere. I reject such ideas of coercion just as I reject a paternalistic alternative.

Moreover, even a reformist must realize that gross economic and social inequality make political equality an illusion. The tradition of my own political thought forbids me to underestimate what can be done for large sections of society, in given conditions, by the adjustment of interests. Experience tells me not to avoid a tough conflict if it is forced upon one, but to look conscientiously at what can be done for the good of one's people, or the disadvantaged classes among them, by means of negotiation, persuasion, and efforts at adjustment.

My friends in the Third World must understand that we over here have to strive for a receptive attitude in those who do not, subjectively, see themselves as exploiters, and are not about to let dubious arguments persuade them that they have a very great deal on their consciences.

We certainly do have to face the fact that the peoples of the colonial and semi-colonial countries have been defrauded. However, many of those to whom I turn in our own part of the world are not bloodsuckers first and foremost, but understand the significance of social reforms. They want to know what international reforms will mean for them. A new North–South policy will win broad support only if it contains an element of healthy self-interest over and above the appeal to our common humanity.

I know the objection raised by many who speak for the South: they are tired of being imposed on and humiliated, and would like to get right out of 'the system'. But all probability suggests that getting out, detaching themselves from the system, will lead to disillusion and further collapse. Let us make use of every chance we get for practical cooperation – the possible spread of excessive harmony in the process is a negligible risk for a clear conscience to take.

My Commission's reports are based on the concept of mutual dependence. We were convinced that the era when one could simply say 'the rich must help the poor' was past. Today we realize that the developing countries are entitled to the just proceeds of their labour and their exports, and not merely on humanitarian grounds. Also that the industrial nations would be well advised to cooperate with them in a reasonable manner, for their own and the common good.

The number of responsible people who have adopted the idea of mutual dependence as their own, rather than simply paying it lip service, may have grown but is not enough to swing the balance. However, more people are now aware of our inter-dependence than was the case a few years ago. Their jobs, their supplies of foodstuffs and energy, even the stability of the banks in which they keep their usually modest accounts, all these depend upon the health of the world economy.

My colleagues and I said that the definition of 'mutual interests' was not an adequate basis for the necessary changes. With an eye to those who are particularly disadvantaged, we emphasize the obligation of promoting international justice. Only a new spirit of solidarity, founded on respect for our own and the common good, will help to smooth the way for the necessary practical solutions. Adjustment, and the sacrifice that adjustment entails, are inevitable if gross injustices are to be abolished – between as well as within states. In the long run no nation or group of nations will save itself by dominating others or by isolating itself.

The other simple realization is that starving people are not free. Nations need bread *and* freedom. This concise solution was proffered decades ago by my Peruvian friend Haya de la Torre and other leaders of social democracy in Latin America.

The unemployed, the 'new poor', or those who are otherwise disadvantaged cannot be expected to be receptive to the problems of the developing countries – unless they do realize that projects are under way, or soon to be under way, which are also in their own interests. In any case, appeals to the guilty conscience easily fall on deaf ears when directed at those who are not in positions of power, and have only a very limited share in decision-making about the future of their country.

And should the guilty conscience stir, it is easily quieted by luxury and extravagance, irresponsibility and corruption, which flourish on a large scale in the South as well as here in the North. Thus it is not surprising that new élites have established them-selves in the South beside or instead of the old ones. Today they frequently profit by their activities on behalf of foreign or multi-national companies. There is certainly no less marked a propensity to despotism and self-enrichment in the governmental, party and military bureaucracies of many of the 'new' states than elsewhere.

After the terrible disarray which German history presented to the world not so long ago, we do well not to wag a reproving finger at our Third World partners. But there is no reason why legitimate doubts should not be expressed. A dialogue between North and South must be open on both sides. As to whether an indiscriminate increase in the developing countries' association with the great industrial nations is really in their best interests, that is another question. We have object lessons which teach us not to make light of the industrial countries' problems of adjustment. But politicians supporting certain kinds of order – the organizers of madness! – are bent on opposing proposals which they label as 'planned economy' and, as already mentioned, 'global Keynesianism'. My old friend Bruno Kreisky, for many years Chancellor of Austria, had a similar experience. At the very beginning of the Seventies, when the effects of a serious world-wide rise in unemployment were being felt, he suggested tying up European industrial plant which was lying idle with the African need for infrastructure. Back came the prompt objection that financing such plans would inevitably have inflationary consequences. Lack of imagination and a pathological aversion to planned projects won the day, and the chance was lost.

The rhetorically not uncommon cliché whereby we are all said to be in the same boat provokes a legitimate question as to who is steering it, and who is just there to row. I do not myself fear that the weight of interests involved will inevitably deprive demands for far-reaching reforms of their moral quality. I think there is still plenty of room for humanitarian commitment to helping one's fellow men and women. Moreover, gestures of disinterested charity are not the only things that count in this world. But our own interests will suffer if we fail to understand the interests of others.

To the surprise of many in the Federal Republic of Germany, it turned out, in a poll taken in the summer of 1984, that 57 per cent of voters felt personal concern over the poverty and hunger of the

Third World. Perhaps word had spread, among some of those canvassed, that the funds allocated to the much-disparaged purpose of development aid were not just being thrown out of the window. The annual report of the World Bank Group said that for every Deutschmark provided by Bonn, DM 1.81 flowed back into German exporting firms. That comes to over DM 100 billion from public funds in the last three decades – a considerable sum, though in the opinion of a considerable minority an inadequate expression of responsibility for our fellow men. And there is another figure we should remember too: we spend rather more per head per year on flowers than we spend on public development aid.

5. Peace at Risk

It is said that in the whole history of warfare, exceptionally dangerous weapons have never gone off of their own accord. I would not rely on that. History has never before known a period in which there has been such comprehensive and thorough worldwide preparation for war.

The Cold War has hinged to a great extent on control of the Third World. World power has never been so concentrated, yet the great powers have never been so unable to establish world *order*. Political thought has seldom been so far from the level of scientific and technological development.

The remark, repeatedly heard, that nuclear means of mass annihilation would never be used, but were merely serving the cause of mutual deterrence, is not very reassuring, since it does not take human and technical failure into account. And why should one suppose that the ever-increasing extent of destructive potential is a suitable way of reducing the idea of the use of those means of destruction to absurdity?

It is worth taking another look at the dimensions. When the Geneva negotiations failed in the autumn of 1983, experts estimated that around 40,000 nuclear weapons – some said 50,000 – had built up in the arsenals of the two superpowers, with a destructive power a million times that of the bomb dropped on

Hiroshima. Experts might argue as to whether it was now possible to extinguish every human life six, seven or eight times over. Europe was experiencing a long period of peace. But nothing could get around the simple realization that the development of modern weaponry had brought vast and hitherto unknown risks into being.

- The fact that modern engines of destruction could go into action independently, through technical error or human failure, cannot really be dismissed in deceptively reassuring terms much longer, and it cannot be repeated often enough.
- The increasing militarization of the developing countries is a cause of rising insecurity.
- In addition, we shall also have the consequences of the race which is now beginning for the militarization of outer space.
- Scientists are in no doubt that the northern hemisphere at least would be plunged into a 'nuclear winter' after an attack by nuclear weapons. Food supplies, the economic system, transport and health services would break down, not only in those areas directly hit, but in other parts of the earth as well. Many species of plants and animals would disappear. It is probable, but not certain, that mankind would be among the species entirely wiped out by a nuclear war.
- A study commissioned by the Pentagon has come to the conclusion that a nuclear conflict between East and West would cause a drop in temperature by as much as 25 degrees, and lasting months.
- Other studies have concluded that even a small-scale nuclear war would set off the 'winter effect', condemning a large part of the world to starve to death. Some forms of life would survive nuclear war: weeds, and worms living on the sea-bed.

I do not doubt that humanity – including political leaders in the East and West and South – would *like* to survive. That does not mean it *will* survive. Peace is not an original condition: we have to 'make' peace and safeguard it. It may be the aim of all systems of belief and basic philosophical attitudes, but it is contrary to all historical experience and to our knowledge of human nature to suppose that such unanimity would prevent war.

In all the argument about the risks to peace it is easy to overlook the fact that the peace with which we are dealing is maintained in the midst of war. Since 1945, there have been over 120 armed conflicts in the Third World – seldom without foreign intervention, and claiming millions of victims, all as a result of 'conventional' warfare.

The realization that a nuclear war could mean the suicide of humanity, to many of us not an entirely new one, goes largely undisputed today. But our ability to make the earth uninhabitable is a new factor. In Africa, too, changes in weather and climate would make agricultural production impossible. In other developing countries not directly affected, the lives of most human beings would also be threatened.

Universal war would entail universal destruction. Its prevention should therefore be a universal duty. But what had Pierre Trudeau, Prime Minister of Canada for many years, to say when he had given up office? The leading politicians of the Western Alliance, he remarked, had almost never touched upon the subject of war and peace in their confidential talks at summit conferences in recent years. . . .

Repeated declarations of willingness to safeguard peace are no longer enough on their own. In view of the state of affairs in which the superpowers have involved themselves, the announcement of peaceful intentions is at best a friendly signal, and in fact falls far short of the requirements of our time. What we need is a well-considered policy in those states and systems which can mobilize sufficient strength and will – in theory and in practice, in the drafting of plans and putting them into effect – in order to reinforce world peace and make it indestructible.

As a step in the right direction, demands for a freeze on nuclear armaments have recently been made: 'A pause, firmly agreed and capable of being monitored, in the testing of new types of nuclear weapons and their launching systems, as well as a similar pause in the deployment of nuclear weapons systems' (Palme Commission, December 1984). Similarly, the Four Continents Initiative, meeting in Delhi in January 1985, in addition called for a freeze on the spread of weapons into outer space.

Slowly, the idea is gaining ground that we shall be able to safeguard peace, now in mortal danger, only *together with* the supposed enemy; that the alleged, and allegedly indispensable, balance of terror must be replaced by a concept of *common* security. To reach this point, and if possible to achieve a balance of good sense and reason, certainly calls for a process of rethinking, since the balance of terror runs counter to all that most people – and those who govern them – believe they know.

The question of credibility has been raised, particularly in Europe: can we rely on such safeguards if there were an emergency destroying what might be defended? Arising from this question, a transitional stage has been proposed wherein the potential dangers on both sides could be proportionately reduced, and thus lead to mutual security.

And would the idea of common security stand any chance beyond the opposing blocs themselves? Next door to Europe, in the Middle East – which as a danger area is comparable to the Balkans before 1914 – the idea may seem objectively cogent, but will still be hard to put into effect.

Political systems must ask themselves, and be asked, how a policy of security other than one of total deterrence can be drawn up. Serious dialogue calls for a *political* initiative. In the long run, security can be achieved only through political thought and action which considers the interests of both sides in security and in increasing it if possible. Every important step which unnecessarily alarms a potential opponent is a step backwards, creating new problems.

In the long run, security for *one* side cannot be achieved by armaments which reduce the security of the *other* side. Whether we look at developments over the last thirty or ten or five years, we see that in the area of major confrontations and the evolution of weaponry, no side will feel secure, high as it may pitch its own efforts, if the other side feels increasingly insecure.

Any dialogue must start from the realization that co-existence is forced upon the world, and it is more important to organize mutual security than to pursue undeniable ideological differences regardless. Existing differences should not prevent us from cooperating.

Risks to world peace were not reduced but increased in various ways (hard as they may be to assess) by the fact that the East–West conflict and North–South differences have become intertwined. When I spoke on co-existence at Harvard over a quarter of a century ago, I started even then from the premise that the East–West situation had been accompanied and influenced by the North–South situation for years; one day, I forecast, North–South issues could even be superimposed on East–West issues.

We have not yet reached that point. It has been shown repeatedly that the main danger to world peace still proceeds from the excessive rivalries of the superpowers. However, that indubitably increases the risk that the East–West conflict will continue intruding into the Third World, with unfortunate effects, and that many Third World countries will be drawn into the arms race between the great powers. Some are only too glad to let themselves be drawn in.

The militarization of the Third World is certainly not just the result of outside influence. Unresolved political and social problems play a considerable part in the setting up of military régimes. But such régimes are then generally incapable of mastering the social, political and economic tasks they face. The area in which they usually fail most conspicuously is that of agricultural production and the processing of agricultural products.

Their commitments in the Third World have not brought much joy to either of the world powers over the last few years. They have not achieved lasting success: either in Iran or Afghanistan, or in their tug-of-war for the Indian subcontinent; or in the strategic plays made for either the Middle East or North-East Africa; nor in the Gulf War, which started at the end of 1980 with American weapons on one side and Soviet weapons on the other; while Central America shows how badly imaginary dangers can lead them astray.

The militarization of the Third World is linked with – or derives its impetus from – extensive exports of weapons, also described as 'military development aid', from industrial nations headed by the superpowers.

That more and more weapons make the world not more but

less secure has yet to make its impact, especially among the majority of those who bear responsibility for the Third World countries. Arsenals of weapons are still being stockpiled in many developing countries, mostly for reasons of prestige. We in Europe or elsewhere in the industrialized world should, however, beware of expressing our indignation too vehemently. For we have not set the Third World a very good example. Far from it: in a great many cases the colonial powers have left both the heritage of old and the germ of new conflicts behind them. Variants of the Cold War have been exported. And not only armaments firms but our governments too have played an extremely active part in the trade in engines of destruction.

6. *Indira's Legacy*

When I saw Indira Gandhi for the last time, in the early summer of 1984 – in the same garden at whose gate she died a few months later – she made a more urgent impression on me than ever before: when, she asked, would Europeans be ready and able to undertake joint action with major powers from the ranks of the non-aligned countries? What action? Bringing mutual pressure to bear on the superpowers! To what end? To find a common denominator for the subjects of the arms race and the international economy! How? By planning a summit conference, and preparing for it without delay.

I am not concerned here to pay tribute to the political achievements of Nehru's daughter, or to examine the criticisms levelled at her by her opponents in their time. I will concentrate on that remarkable woman's legacy to international politics:

• In March 1983, at the Delhi conference, Indira Gandhi, on behalf of India, was appointed to chair the non-aligned countries' movement. She defined it as 'the greatest peace movement in history'. Its programme, she said, was one of independence, freedom, and equality between nations. The closing 'political declaration on disarmament, survival and co-existence in the age of nuclear weapons' bore her stamp.

- In the spring of 1984, Indira Gandhi took up the Four Continents Initiative, which has been continued by her son and successor Rajiv. Together with Presidents Alfonsín of Argentina, de la Madrid of Mexico and Nyerere of Tanzania, as well as Prime Ministers Palme of Sweden and Papandreou of Greece, India appealed to the superpowers to put an end to the arms race. Along with a large number of parliamentary representatives from many lands, I associated myself with this appeal. Julius Nyerere said, with the approval of us all: 'Peace is too important to be left to the White House and the Kremlin.'

- Indira Gandhi had concentrated more on North–South than East–West questions at the conference of non-aligned countries. She expressed the sense of disappointment that two decades had passed without any progress being made in the reorganization of international economic relations. (This choice of subject also had the advantage of helping to play down political differences within the non-aligned countries. The influence of a sometimes obtrusively one-sided prejudice against the USA was considerably reduced. One quarter of the participants inclined more or less towards the Soviet Union; half did not want to commit themselves.)

- The Prime Minister of India had appointed a group of experts from the non-aligned countries to prepare a report on urgent monetary and financial issues at the end of 1983; it was ready in July 1984, and was intended as the preliminary to a high-level conference in India in the autumn of 1985. Mrs Gandhi believed that 'if you leave a problem on the technical plane too long it can easily get lost in detail'. Thus, one must raise the subject to the plane of international politics, and only those chiefly responsible were in a position to do so (an assumption which admittedly said more for her notable self-confidence than her assessment of her colleagues).

- In our conversations of June 1984, in which the present Prime Minister Rajiv Gandhi took part, we discussed the connection between détente and cooperation. In Delhi, as on my preceding visit to Peking, the questions asked about the path Europe was taking and her ability to accept new forms of cooperation were sometimes of a hopeful, sometimes of an impatiently insistent nature. Our mutual friend Shridath Ramphal, the Commonwealth Secretary-General, had said, not long before, that a coalition of the medium-sized powers in East and West, North and South was needed: a coalition aiming for peace, more sensible regulation of the world economy, and preservation of the natural environment. In concrete terms, it was a matter of how a dialogue between interested powers could be initiated at a high level and lead to a summit conference as soon as possible.

- All this coincided with the way other people were thinking, so that at every stage of my Latin American tour in the autumn of 1984, I was asked to support the idea of an international meeting at the highest level, to take place within the foreseeable future, on the subject of disarmament and development, and in particular on ways to overcome the debt crisis: a conference on the model of Cancun.*

In Delhi, we were agreed that if safeguarding world peace had become the prime target, then not only must something be done to counteract the arms race and heightened East–West tensions; it was even more important to abolish those dangers arising from poverty in large parts of the world. Famine in the poverty belts of Africa and Asia will not leave the better-fed parts of our planet unaffected for ever. Where millions go hungry, we cannot regard peace as genuinely secured. Overcoming hunger is the most elementary of human needs. The efforts of the international community must be concentrated upon this issue.

Safeguarding peace, protecting the environment, and organizing economic relations sensibly are the most important tasks that we and the next generation have to face. The struggle to overcome world famine is still the most urgent challenge to our common humanity.

I belong to a generation that has learned more than once in its lifetime how war brings hunger in its wake and can lead on to famine. Are we so sure that a future generation will be spared this experience in reverse? Is it really a mistake to suppose that hunger can lead to war? Or that the peoples of the northern half of the planet, having succumbed to despair, may simply blow the whole

* Cancun was the scene of the summit meeting held at the suggestion of the Brandt Commission in October 1981, on the Atlantic coast of Mexico.

thing up some day? Or that as the population grows apace, misery may lead to chaos, unleash terror, and bring armed conflict in its wake?

I am told that people on the brink of starvation do not look for a fight. But history can show us examples to the contrary. And as to the future, it is nowhere written that people cannot revolt in great numbers instead of dying in silence. I agreed with something I read in a major weekly journal: 'It is true that the hungry are seldom aggressive. But can we rely on the apathy of the poor once their own forests have been cut down, their own soil cropped to death, the foundations of their own lives undermined?'

In January 1984, at a joint meeting in Rome of the members of my Commission and the Commission on Disarmament and Security, under the chairmanship of Olof Palme, which had then published its report, we stated that in view of growing economic pressure and social crises, the political instability of Third World countries might well increase, involving other powers – with the eventual risk of a nuclear war, from whose consequences no country would be safe. Greater military competition, we said, was making the economic pressure worse. . . .

In June 1982, the report of the Palme Commission said that all states would suffer if expenditure on armaments were to undermine the economic welfare of those nations with a particularly heavy involvement in international trade. Everyone would suffer if the drain on national finances for arms purposes were to endanger foreign aid or development loans. Mutual security, said the Commission, could not be set apart from a course leading towards economic recovery and the concept of mutual prosperity.

Mass poverty *can* lead to war. Where hunger rules, peace has no firm footing. In the report of my Commission we said we did not believe that the world could live in peace, or that prosperity could continue indefinitely even in the North, if large areas of the South, with hundreds of millions of people, were excluded from all real prospect of progress and left alone on the brink of survival.

That war can lead to economic redistribution is not unfamiliar in contemporary thought. A French friend of mine, former Minister of Agriculture Michel Rocard, has said that if populations grow at a faster rate than the necessities of life, and if it is decided, in the name of liberalism, that there must be no state intervention, then there are parts of the world where the future of humanity will entail revolutions and military solutions.

Elsewhere, I have read that the destruction of the soil, the rivers and forests could become a major cause of political and military instability – which could lead to revolutions and perhaps to war. In any case, it does not take much imagination to envisage the growth of hatred among many of those who are forced to live in hunger and want through no fault of their own.

We need not listen to those callous bureaucrats employed in politics or economics who will not discuss simple truths, or who bury them in a mass of trivialities. Even supposing concern over armaments development and the waste of resources it entails were exaggerated – we are still left to wonder why it should not be possible to set aside some percentage of expenditure on arms, and why the nations of the world are incapable of so doing, in order to use the funds thus diverted for practical purposes that would promote peace, and abolish mass hunger and severe poverty.

We may assume that in 1986 over $1,000 billion will be spent, globally, on military purposes. Development aid as recorded by the international organizations adds up to less than 5 per cent of that vast sum. It is hard to see why at least 5 per cent, i.e. one-twentieth of world expenditure on armaments – in addition to present development aid – should not be used to overcome world hunger and on projects of economic cooperation. (Five years ago it was worked out that even 0.5 per cent could provide agricultural equipment to improve the agrarian production of most of the poor countries so much within a decade that they could feed themselves.)

At this point I ought to mention that there are no absolutely unanimous estimates of international expenditure on arms. But the trend is clear. The very reputable Stockholm International Peace Research Institute (SIPRI) estimates a figure lower than my assumed $1,000 billion. I am going by a study made by the US Arms Control and Disarmament Authority (ACDA), according to which a good $970 billion was spent on armaments purposes in 1984, NATO and the Warsaw Pact countries being responsible for three-quarters of that sum. Authoritative British circles have come to similar conclusions. (A slight reduction in the *increase* of the American defence budget for 1986, should such a reduction occur, would scarcely alter the overall picture.)

Meanwhile we have studies to soothe us – and where do we not? If arms expenditure were frozen (in the West), we are told, we would not see any improvement in the international economy for another twenty years, and moreover there is no indication that the arms race is 'completely out of control'. . . .

Years ago, I countered that attitude with some comparisons which are still relevant today:

- The military expenditure of half a day would be enough to finance the World Health Organization's programme to eradicate malaria.
- The money a modern tank costs could improve storage facilities for 100,000 tonnes of rice, so that annual wastage of 4,000 tonnes or more would be avoided – a day's ration for eight million people.
- The same sum would be enough to provide 1,000 classrooms for 30,000 schoolchildren.
- The price of a fighter plane would equip 40,000 village pharmacies.
- And my colleagues added this example: the price of a new nuclear submarine is equivalent to the education budgets of 23 developing countries with 160 million children of school age.

I am impressed to find how openly it is now being said, even by financial experts and leading bankers, that only an end to the arms race will extricate us from our common crisis. At the same time the connection between the arms race and the world economy, which strikes an instinctive chord in us, could do with more detailed scientific illumination. To the normal human mind, it is perfectly plain that social wealth is being devoured by armaments, while lacking elsewhere. Even scientific analysis will not reveal otherwise.

Meanwhile, time is running out. We are said to be approaching midnight, and I am afraid that is indeed the case. But I also think we should understand the full meaning of the French riddle about the nature of 'exponential growth'. In a pond of waterlilies, the riddle goes, there is a single leaf. Every day the number of leaves doubles – two leaves on the second day, four on the third day, eight on the fourth day, etc. 'If the pond is full on the thirtieth day,' the question runs, 'when is it half full?' Answer: 'On the twenty-ninth day.'

II

NO LAUGHING MATTER

I have learned just *how* far apart North and South are – from the fact that there are hardly any political jokes on the subject. Unsavoury racist humour will not be expected of me. I have grave doubts of a joke such as the one about the President of X-land applying to the World Bank for a loan to build prisons 'to replace the colonial institutions'. Or the one about another President who orders the well-publicized founding of a Communist Party, to make aid from Washington more probable. Or the one about the Soviet Republic said to have sent snowploughs to Africa because that was what its plan provided for. But there is more than a grain of truth in all such cases, though one may not want to believe it.

It was very different with East–West relations, even, or particularly, in the most difficult periods of the Cold War. I have vivid memories of such humour from my time in Berlin, and during my years in government in Bonn – and in the Foreign Service – I had aides who could be relied upon to make me laugh with jokes from the Eastern European capitals. An attempt to do any such thing with North–South relations would not have been very successful. The explanation is not just a matter of geographical distance. Despite all the extremes of ideological conflict between East and West, we were still on the same wavelength.

And yet a little humour, albeit wry, may help our theme.

- When the Secretariat of my Commission was working in Geneva, I met an amiable ex-President of the Swiss Confederation in the Valais. He asked the purpose of my repeated visits to the Lake of Geneva. I told him about the report on which we were working. The ex-President's unexpected reaction was: 'North–South? Ah, yes, the Italians as usual. . . .'

46

- Not so many years ago, a newly elected President of the USA was asked his opinion of marihuana. He replied that the freedom of that country would be defended to the last drop of blood. (When I told this joke in Bonn, a friend added, with some malice, that the affiliated party in Marihuana had probably joined the Socialist International by now.)

- In Geneva, an African friend told us that they had a new saying in his country, 'Human rights begin with breakfast', adapted from the English expression, 'Charity begins at home'.

- One scholar asks another: who is even worse off than a small farmer in a poor country? Answer: the farmer's wife.

- In an argument about development politics, an American was trying to contradict the complacent observation that omelettes can't be turned back into eggs (or that one can't have one's cake and eat it too). He called for a more sensible approach. 'Broken eggs will make perfectly good omelettes if you leave the pan on the stove, and you have some herbs and you've beaten the eggs properly – but not if you throw them on the floor.'

- During a visit to Kuwait, our colleague Al Hamad, then his country's Finance Minister, was satirizing all the talk that goes on about partnership and dubious joint ventures. The chicken proposes a joint venture to the pig. The pig asks what they are going to produce together. Ham and eggs, says the chicken. To which the pig replies: 'Yes, but while you'll get off lightly with making a daily contribution, I shall be asked for total commitment.'

- A Pakistani acquaintance remarked, more ironically than aggressively, that there can be only one thing worse than being exploited by capitalists, and that is not being exploited at all.

- A clever Russian woman wrote that she would reserve for her two worst enemies the hunger of the starving and the repletion of the satisfied.

- At a conference in Rome, the Tanzanian Minister of Agriculture recollected one of the sayings of his country: 'If you see a lion, you won't save yourself by standing still and praying. You must run and pray instead, pray for the strength to go on running.'

- When I was awarded the Third World Prize, and was reminded of the influence of East–West on North–South relations, an

47

East African colleague contributed a metaphor from his native language, Swahili: 'When the elephants fight the grass suffers.' 'And when they make love,' someone else added, 'it would suffer even worse.'

- Marek Halter makes Solomon show surprise at Abraham's remark that one should *not* acknowledge one's friends in their need. 'Don't you understand?' asks Abraham. 'Suppose a white man happens to be beating a slave. What do you do to help the slave? You stop the man beating him, and then you turn back to your own business with a sense of great satisfaction. But the slave is still enslaved.'

- Bruno Kreisky and I were discussing the Argentinian Minister for Economic Affairs, his immense problems and his plan – later dropped – simply to suspend payment of interest on the country's heavy burden of debt. 'That reminds me of the two men in Czernovitz,' said Kreisky. 'One was very downcast, told the other he couldn't go on any longer, and why not: he had debts everywhere and could pay none of them, so he must put an end to his existence. The other man advised him not to do anything in too much of a hurry, since there was generally some way out to be found. Two weeks later he met his acquaintance, the man who had wanted to commit suicide. He was now warbling merrily and twirling his cap on top of his walking-stick. "What's come over you?" says the other man. "Why this change?" "Well," says the first man, "I've been round all my creditors, starting with the grocer and ending with my land-lord. I've told them all I can't give them any money, not now and not later. So now it's *their* problem. . . ."'

III

ALL THE PEOPLE AND THEIR DAILY BREAD

1. *An Unsatisfactory Balance Sheet*

North–South relations have not been making progress in the last few years, least of all in the poorest countries. To the contrary: warnings have been disregarded, even modest hopes have remained unfulfilled. Instead, we have seen the confirmation of many gloomy forecasts contained in the first report of my North–South Commission, published early in 1980. We were accused of pessimism at the time. If only that accusation had proved correct! But in fact it turns out that:

- The number of people suffering from malnutrition is still 500 million, and the number of those living in 'absolute poverty' around 800 million. These figures represent no deterioration, relatively speaking, only if we take into account the fact that world population is growing faster than the vast group of those who live a life of extreme destitution.
- At present, enough food is being produced worldwide. There is a greater supply of foodstuffs than for many years past, and international food reserves have grown – but famine disasters such as the African catastrophes still occur. Every minute, thirty children die for lack of food and clean water.
- The energy crisis seems to *us* to have slackened, but there is an increasingly acute shortage of firewood; this is the poor countries' real energy crisis.
- The threat to the forests and to water, the spread of deserts and exhausted soil, clearly show how great an ecological breakdown will face those who come after us.

- The export to the Third World of the East–West conflict, and the increasing militarization of the Third World, severely encumber the development process, as I have already shown, and mean the waste of a great deal of money that could be more productively employed, as well as the waste of talents and creative minds which might help to solve more meaningful problems. (It is estimated that out of every 1,000 scientists all over the world, 200 are occupied with research into arms technology.)
- We are facing a massive debt crisis, one of an order my Commission forecast at an early stage; I do not say so smugly.
- The further increase in trade barriers that we feared has come about – protectionism triumphant in defiance of all assurances to the contrary from official government sources.
- And more than one country is already shaken by social unrest. This is the consequence of the international crisis, and the reaction to traditional programmes for overcoming the *symptoms* of crisis.

It may be over-hasty to say that the real, acute crisis is actually upon us, for in the strict sense of the word, crisis means the state immediately preceding collapse or the beginning of recovery. I do not agree with those who believe that we are already over the critical phase, in that sense. I decidedly do not agree with them, for behind the obvious problems there looms the danger of the total extinction of life on earth.

When is the time to make the most strenuous possible of intellectual and political efforts, if not now? We are preparing to operate upon the very germ cells of Nature, we are playing Fate. So we are also, though in a very different way, responsible for our Fate. Either we live together in peace – at peace with our neighbours and with Nature – or we shall perish together.

Contrasts and contradictions mark the face of this world, and do so to an increasing degree. We have fundamentally changed the world. To a certain extent it has become smaller – particularly through new means of transport and communications technology, but also through our means of destruction. If we do not wish to decline entirely into becoming the agents of a destructive process, we must change our view of the world and our mental attitudes.

More cooperation, mutual security, mutual solutions to the problems of employment and the environment are all required, and indeed are imperative, but we still fall short even of those forms of cooperation which have already been achieved. Many of us resort to old remedies to cure new diseases. But only if we grasp the dangerous reality of our times can we hope to take any joint action to ensure that there will be a future.

2. *Over Ten Billion People?*

The catchphrase of 'population *explosion*' is no exaggeration. In a single generation, humanity has doubled its numbers. Every five days another million are born. In 1950 there were 2.5 billion people, in 1985 there are nearly 5 billion, by the turn of the century there will be over 6 billion. Those who live to be old enough will see the population of the world tripled within their time.

It would be an illusion to assume that the figure will stabilize at 6 to 8 billion. In the year 2050 there will be some 10 billion people or more – this, of course, is no more than a computation of probability. However, the progressive acceleration factor which has been a feature since the early nineteenth century is an established fact. In 120 years, one billion became two billion. Humanity reached its third billion within 32 years, and its fourth in another 15 years.

If we take the World Bank's development report of the summer of 1984 as a basis, the 6.1 billion people expected to be alive in the year 2000 would then be distributed between the continents as follows: Asia 3,600 million; America 898 million; Africa 828 million; Europe 520 million, the Soviet Union 312 million; Oceania 30 million.

Sceptics, however, observing current events, point out that the population of Africa need not necessarily grow, but could shrink to half its present size within less than a generation. And in the year 2050, again, the picture would look quite different from our assumptions of what it will be at the turn of the century.

Two other pieces of data have been recorded, indicating the course events are taking. Three-quarters of the world population live in today's developing countries, and this imbalance will increase. And on average, 44 per cent of the inhabitants of the developing countries are under 15 years old, as compared to 24 per cent in the industrial countries.

So far, the assumption that the sum of world population will reach equilibrium at 11 to 12 billion in the second half of the next century is pure wishful thinking. No real change of trend can be discerned. On the other hand, estimates of the number of people who can actually live on the earth range from 10 to 40 billion.

There is no doubt that all who are alive today could be fed, and millions more. So I would not call the situation hopeless, but it is certainly serious. And no one can contradict the World Bank when it says that without efficient family planning in the Third World countries, economic and social development will not take place. Robert McNamara, who looked into this matter himself during his time as President of the World Bank, and again spoke out clearly in 1984, goes further than that. He predicts that failure to practise efficient family planning will call authoritarian régimes into being, and those régimes will then take large-scale compulsory measures.

Such a viewpoint has given rise, and still does, to a sense of the urgency of making population policies involving birth control an important subject of international concern, and of advocating provision of the means to carry out this aspect of development policy. That does not mean exporting specific moral attitudes, but a serious approach to a political effort on whose success or failure much depends.

According to the predictions of the report already quoted, in the year 2050 India, with 1.5 billion people, will be the world's most populous nation. China, which has set itself to observe the rule of one-child families, will not be far behind, with an increase in population to 'only' 1.45 billion. What about the rest? There will be 470 million people living in Nigeria, 330 million in Indonesia, 360 million in Bangladesh, 300 million in Pakistan, 280 million in Brazil. I knew Burma and Ethiopia when they had 20 million inhabitants; in the middle of the next century one will have 100 million and the other 165 million. When I first visited

Tanzania (still Tanganyika at the time), the country had some 10 million inhabitants; by 2050 the figure will have grown to around 95 million. The calculations forecast that there will be 150 million people in Vietnam in the year 2050, 180 million in Mexico, 140 million in Iran, and 100 million each in Egypt, Algeria and Turkey.

Urban population is growing at an even faster rate than world population as a whole, especially in the Third World:

- There will be 21 Third World cities with over 10 million inhabitants in the year 2000, 15 of them in Asia: Mexico City will have 31 million, São Paulo 26 million, Shanghai 24 million, Peking 21 million, Rio 19 million, Bombay, Calcutta and Djakarta 17 million each, Seoul 14 million, Cairo and Madras 13 million, Buenos Aires 12 million.
- Other cities coming into the same category will be Tokyo/Yokohama with 24 million, New York with 22 million and Greater Los Angeles with 14 million.
- In twenty years' time, half of all Americans will be living in cities with over a million inhabitants, while the flow of people towards the big cities will continue all over the world.
- Conglomerations so huge that one can hardly grasp the extent of them are developing in the Third World. One wonders what will become of those squalid settlements known as *favelas* in Brazil, *barrios* in Mexico and *ranchos* in Venezuela, where redevelopment, if any, is making little progress.

Who would accuse those who hear the time bombs ticking away in cities, countries and regions of panic-mongering? The fact that a reduction in our own West German population is forecast for the next decade does not cheer me. Still, we might think ourselves lucky if that were our only worry. I know those who, all things considered, would be glad to change places with us. We need not fear the downfall of the West as yet. I am assuming that the Europeans – and within Europe, the Germans – still have something to offer the world.

The fear that 'they' in the South are to be kept down, while 'we' in the North only want to maintain our economic lead, has taken firm root in the minds of many Third World leaders. Many of them have thought, or still think, that a large population represents a power factor. There are also cultural, traditional and religious reasons for rejecting any kind of birth control. And finally, that simple fact expressed in South America by the saying that, 'The beds of poverty are fertile', still holds good. . . .

Only too often, however, population growth is regarded as the chief cause of hunger and destitution in the Third World. People prefer to suppress the connection between industrialism in the North and colonialism in the South. It is easy to forget that in the present state of the world economy, the poor are often too weak to defend themselves from exploitation.

The North and the West have frequently been accused of hypocrisy. It pays your families to have children, say the accusers, you get child allowances and tax relief, and then you want us to limit *our* families. As time has gone by, however, leading sections of the community in many of the poor countries have themselves come to realize that the benefits of an over-abundance of children can become a scourge instead, and that no amount of economic progress is of any use if it is literally more than consumed by excessive population growth.

There is a hint of the reversal of excessive population growth in some African countries. But the labour force of children who can help their parents still counts for a good deal, particularly in rural areas. And in the Third World, having children still represents provision for one's old age, something unobtainable from other sources. None the less, at the United Nations conference held in Mexico in the summer of 1984, which I have already mentioned, the representatives of the developing countries were in favour of expanding family planning programmes and stocking up on family planning material. Ten years earlier, at the first World Population Conference in Bucharest, opinion had not by any means been so decided.

This time, in Mexico, opposition came from the centre of the Catholic Church – and from the United States government. Washington had sent a delegation whose spokesman stated in all seriousness that everything would regulate itself if economic activity was left to go its own way. Economic liberalism as a substitute for contraception? In practical terms, all support for the termination of pregnancies should be withdrawn.

It was not surprising to find that the Vatican was of the same mind. Comments made publicly bore witness to the crisis of conscience obviously suffered by many millions of women and men whose Church is dear to their hearts. It was also reported reliably and uncontroversially that 'a growing number of priests view the conflict of aims between over-population and living conditions commensurate with human dignity with growing concern'. Very probably, contraception and abortion cannot be indefinitely equated in principle; the consequences extend too far beyond the field with which the morality of the Church is concerned.

The World Population Conference of the summer of 1984, however, made some meaningful recommendations; soothing reassurances had been granted in advance to the USA delegation, and – for the sake of peace – the Soviet delegation was conceded a passage relating to a policy of peace. And yet the President of Mexico, hosting the conference, had spoken out with refreshing bluntness against trivialization of the subject. The lowering of the birth rate, he said, was dependent on the resources available in the fields of nutrition, health, employment and education. My Commission had argued along the same lines.

Experience has long taught us that drawing up and equipping family planning programmes will be of limited efficacy if those programmes do not go hand in hand with the development of community life in villages or towns; higher social status for women; and better chances of survival for babies.

No nation has ever yet known its birth rate to fall without a previous drop in the mortality rate. Anything that helps to overcome poverty and promote better health makes a vital contribution to keeping the increase in population under control. The higher the proportion of those who can read and write and the greater the progress made towards equality for women, the more striking is the success of family planning programmes. It really does make a difference whether the women of the Nile Valley do or do not believe they will have no sons if they take the Pill, or if it is said elsewhere that the Pill is an invention of the enemies of Islam. The greater the share people have in the economic yield of their own labour, and the more intensively medical care is provided for the newborn, the more noticeably does the birth-rate sink; family planning is most unsatisfactory if it is divorced from a health service. And the sooner those concerned reach a certain level of education (and income), the readier they will be to use the family planning services.

Family planning has made considerable headway in such diverse countries as Colombia and Costa Rica, Korea and Sri Lanka. Even in a large country like Indonesia the number of couples who decide to practise birth control has risen from 3 to 50 per cent. The city states of Hong Kong and Singapore are frequently cited as being particularly successful, though the methods of reward or punishment employed there have met with much criticism. In India, where a sterilization programme was forcefully imposed in the mid-Sixties, the government met strong resistance. The concept of the one-child family decreed by the state in the People's Republic of China encounters understandable objections too; whatever harsh measures may be taken, the population there will still grow by several more hundred million.

It is easy, but not particularly helpful, for certain European resolutions to call for an end to the population explosion, while simultaneously maintaining that one should not encroach too far upon the rights of individuals to decide the size of their families. It is irresponsible to let things drift, in the name of a misunderstood notion of freedom, if population increases faster than the prospective means of subsistence. This is particularly true where countries trying to develop have their chances of development curtailed from outside.

3. All Could Be Fed

With our present opportunities for producing food, more people than are now living on the earth could be fed. However, the gap between the reproduction of human children and the production of the means to feed them is wider in some regions than others. So the question is, how can agriculture be made profitable? And how are the poor to be able to buy what they desperately need? And how are the export interests of large firms or of the state to be subordinated to basic domestic consumption? It makes no sense to export foodstuffs from countries where millions of people do not have enough to eat.

When global food production declined slightly a few years ago, the authorities responsible declared that the world food situation as a whole was not endangered. That makes the dreadful figures I am about to set out here no better. It is important to recognize the inconsistency of a state of affairs in which the international supply situation is comparatively better than it used to be, while at the same time whole regions are stricken by famine.

Let us recall those round numbers: over 500 million children and adults suffering from chronic malnutrition, over 800 million living in conditions of 'absolute poverty' – such was the estimate made by World Bank experts a few years ago. Their idea was to obtain points of reference for the large number of people who are barely able to survive, owing to a combination of undernourishment, disease, illiteracy, high birth-rates, under-employment, and tiny incomes. In 1979, according to the World Bank's estimates, there were about 800 million people in this category, as already mentioned, most of them in southern Asia and in sub-Saharan Africa. An estimate for 1985 would not look much better. There are varying forecasts of figures for the year 2000: in unfavourable circumstances, there would be a further rise from 800 to 1,000 million; in better circumstances, the figure might drop to about 600 million. A large part of humanity is thus affected by 'absolute poverty' in intellectual as well as physical development; many are condemned to perish miserably.

No, world hunger is not a hysterical flight of fancy. It cannot be argued away, nor can it be made to disappear by magic; at best it can be repelled, with much effort. The question is: practically and morally, how long can those immediately affected endure it, and how long can the rest of us endure it? I have already linked it with the waste of public funds on other purposes, and with issues of international security.

Let the experts debate the precise line to be drawn between chronic malnutrition and absolute poverty. The appalling pictures from East Africa made a deep impression on us laymen. Yet not a dozen years before, pictures no less shocking had appeared in illustrated magazines and on our television screens, pictures from the Sahel zone in general and Ethiopia in particular; and from Bangladesh, and Cambodia, where there has been much misuse of international aid.

Many who saw those pictures from Ethiopia were overwhelmed by bitter memories – memories of 1945 and the skeletal figures emerging from concentration camps. I was reminded of a friend of mine, a Norwegian doctor interned in Sachsenhausen as a deportee, who had to bear the burden of deciding which patients in the infirmary were to get a chance of survival and which were not. I thought of him when I heard what was said by the nurses and emergency doctors who had to make similarly hard decisions at the gates of the Ethiopian camps; only a few children could be let in. One German nurse wrote: 'What I hate most is the moment when people have to be sorted out. I feel like a judge on life and death: one child gets a chance, another is condemned to die.'

> In 1984, James Grant, director of UNICEF, stated that the numbers of children dying before their fifth birthday, from malnutrition and largely preventable illnesses, were:
> - 15 million a year
> - 41,000 a day
> - 28 a minute

Mr Grant of UNICEF sees family planning as 'the best method of preventing the death of some 20,000 babies and small children a day'. None the less, there has been a distinct drop in child mortality in a number of developing countries during the last three decades. Looking at the world as a whole, it can be said, and this is very pleasing, that for rather more than a generation, there has been no rise in the number of children who do not have enough to eat and no clean water, and who at the same time are growing up without a minimum of educational and medical care. We may even speak of a declining trend. But the rapid increase in population, linked to environmental disasters and economic distress, could reverse that trend again at any time.

It is not just the situation in Africa that has come to a head. In India, despite a general improvement in food supplies, the health of a large part of the population is still threatened by inadequate nutrition. The same applies to other parts of Africa, and it still applies – or now applies again – to many people in Latin America.

Whether 12 or 15 million children are dying of starvation a year, whether 500 or 800 million people in the world go hungry, there is an individual fate behind every set of figures, however neatly rounded it may be: the fate of a human being with a right to life, a right not to be harmed, a right to a dignified existence.

Instead, a vast number are denied the simplest right a human being has, the right to live. This need not be so, and it would not be so if nations and their governments and the international federations could manage material wealth a little more sensibly, help one another rather more in the field of agriculture, and see their international responsibility to their fellow men writ a little larger.

The fate of every starving human being is a crime against the values, principles and aims by which many of us who do not go hungry claim to live, by which our governments claim to pursue their policies, and which are invoked at international confer-ences. Despair and rancour are growing in the minds of many who feel that all this need not be as it is. Even in those countries whose people are well fed, indignation is rising at the inadequate action being taken, the incompetence of civil servants and the indifference of humanity. The suffering is being discussed and accounted for. But action to relieve that suffering is either not taken at all, or is on too small a scale, or comes too late.

Unfortunately there are bureaucrats, including some in the diplomatic services, who will let any human feeling cool down until nothing remains of the initial impulse, however well meant, but a troublesome duty. I remember a conference of the Council of Europe. A minister from Northern Europe had been going to come and speak. He was unable to attend, and an ambassador was delegated to read out what had been conveyed to him as the minister's speech. It turned out that the speech was not even at an advanced draft stage, and contained nothing that had not been said before. The meeting was running out of time, but the ambassador, a man on the brink of retirement, insisted on delivering the speech, making matters no better by his soporific style of delivery. One wonders what such people can achieve when they do not just have to deliver speeches from their own ministries, but must negotiate difficult issues with actual Third World representatives, and when, this being the vital point, they are supposed to do something effective at home!

But are there still grounds for hope, all the same? The mere repetition of what may sound over-optimistic will not do. Everyone could be fed *if*. . . . And we must not dwell on superficial comparisons. Many of the developing countries start out from a less favourable situation than did those countries which went through their industrial revolution in the last century. None the less, I affirm my conviction that the task of feeding humanity can be solved, and can be solved primarily by agricultural reforms in the respective regions concerned.

Over and beyond that, biotechnology will open up opportunities of which we had no conception until quite recently. The next question is whether new methods of converting and storing solar energy can be put to work quickly enough, before the firewood disaster gets out of hand, and whether a breakdown of the water supply can be averted, and satisfactory use of sea-water made for economic purposes. I think both of these are possible.

In the autumn of 1974, with the famine disasters in the Sahel zone and Bangladesh still fresh in people's minds, World Food Day was announced at an international conference, and a rallying cry went out: within ten years, it was said, no child should go hungry. Some years ago, when I was to speak in Rome on the occasion of World Food Day, at the invitation of FAO (the United Nations Food and Agriculture Organization), I thought it would be appropriate, yet still rather bold, to extend that deadline just a little: 'By the end of this century, may humanity see the day when children need no longer go to bed hungry, when families need no longer wonder where tomorrow's food is coming from, and the future of humanity is no longer crippled by malnutrition.'

Will those who are young enough to prepare for a new century really see that day? Always supposing such a path is still open to humanity. . . .

4. *Hunger in Africa*

Two 'poverty belts' were described in the report of the Brandt Commission. One stretched across Africa from the Sahara to the northern banks of Lake Nyasa, the other from North and South Yemen and Afghanistan eastwards through South Asia and some of the East Asian countries. It can still be said that unless energetic and precisely defined measures are taken to improve agriculture, 'the Eighties and Nineties could bring even worse scenes of hunger than the Seventies. . . .'

That estimate has not proved false or exaggerated either. However, a correction should be made with regard to Africa: countries south of Lake Nyasa too, particularly Mozambique, are now suffering severely from food shortages. The same applies to a number of countries on the western side of the continent, such as Angola.

FAO's warning system forecast food shortages for 24 African countries, in essence as the result of drought. FAO has been criticized for not relating the warning clearly and urgently enough to Ethiopia. But criticisms are also made when the problems of a region seen as a whole are pushed into the background because of an acute crisis in one of its countries. We might, however, have expected those governments affected, and to that extent responsible, to be better informed about the vital problems of their countries, and more intensively concerned with them, than was the case in Addis Ababa and elsewhere.

Aid for Ethiopia took a long time to get under way. Its efficacy was impaired by the fact that the country, with an 'Eastern-bloc orientated' administration in power, was to a great extent cut off from international development aid, and that those very provinces worst affected by the famine, the northern provinces of Eritrea, Tigré and Wollo, have been arenas of guerrilla warfare for decades. Efforts to get hostilities suspended so that aid could reach all who needed it proved peculiarly difficult; resettlement moves met with criticism because ulterior political motives were suspected of being behind them.

On the other hand, despite all the polemic that went beforehand, this did not prevent the superpowers from acting together to help relieve famine on the spot. Soviet planes carried American

It was said of Ethiopia that:
- Even last time, i.e. in the 1973 disaster, drought and famine claimed 200,000 lives.
- In the first half of 1984, the talk was of 300,000 victims.
- By the end of 1984, it was estimated that of the 600,000 or more people suffering acutely from the famine, half would die.
- The full number of those affected by the famine, according to an estimate made by a UN representative, was said to be several million.

In Africa as a whole (south of the Sahara) we may say that:
- 150 to 450 million are suffering from inadequate nutrition.
- 30 to 35 million face the threat of famine.
- Famine is not just the result of natural disaster, but the consequence of political, economic and ecological mistakes.

wheat: a pleasing picture, like the smooth collaboration of the West German air force with East German units. Peter McPherson, head of the US development agency, specifically welcomed cooperation with the Soviet Union and other Eastern bloc states.

Undoubtedly there are three main causes of the disastrous situation:

1. Serious changes in ecological factors – deforestation, overgrazing, the spread of deserts.
2. Grave mistakes and errors made by the governments concerned, not least in imperial Ethiopia, and an almost incredible neglect of the agricultural sector.
3. A failure of international development policy, just where it ought to have brought about fundamental reforms to encourage agricultural production and supply.

The effect of the climatic change which led to severe drought, with the additional consequences of impoverishment of the soil and the destructive exploitation of forests, can hardly be overestimated.

At the turn of the year between 1984/85, it was calculated that 21 or as many as 27 African countries were stricken by drought. Besides Ethiopia and the Sudan, those particularly hard hit were Chad, Mali, Niger, Mauretania, Uganda and Mozambique, and not least affected were the refugee camps in the Sudan and Somalia. As I write this, it is to be feared that the disaster is not coming to an end but only just beginning.

The simple truth is: Africa south of the Sahara is a single great region where food production per head of the population has declined in the last two decades, and not just because of the catastrophic droughts. And one third of its entire population is undernourished.

What a vast change in the course of only a few decades! Around 1950, the developing countries as a whole, including the African developing countries, were still classed as self-supporting. Over the last few decades, they have needed more and more grain imports. How has this change come about?

The connection between food production and population growth is quite clear: the population of Africa is doubling within 25 years, and even faster in some countries. Nor must we overlook the fact that agrarian commodities have been unwisely exported, because it was in the interests of big business to export,

---

- Forty per cent of Ethiopia was forest at the turn of the century; today, it is only 2.5 per cent.
- The Sahara is extending, by about 150 kilometres to date (or 650,000 square kilometres of arable and grazing land in the last 50 years).
- Considerable parts of the Sahel zone have become semi-desert, with disastrous harvests, lost herds and abandoned villages.
- Extensive soil erosion has led to the clearing of land for cultivation by burning and complete deforestation; every year several more thousand hectares of forest become charcoal or firewood.
- We are seeing more and more emergencies, even in countries which normally have a high rainfall, such as Zaïre, or the countries on the west coast.

---

or exporting seemed advantageous to a country's balance of trade. But there were no funds available to pay for fertilizers and pesticides or agricultural implements; the dollar and oil prices had risen too high. Money for armaments, however, has usually been forthcoming.

One African head of state has observed, self-critically, that Africa's agriculture is sick. Agriculture has been seriously neglected in many of the countries that are now independent. That had to do with the notion of progress which was conveyed to them: industry was a good thing, agriculture not so good, and thus not so important either. And here governments must answer for what they themselves have done or left undone. I surely include in this criticism those who formed 1,000 tribes into 50 states, and provided the dubious models. But matters cannot stop at the allocation of blame. I myself found it helpful to hear how unsparingly an experienced African diplomat took various of his continent's governments to task for their false priorities, ineffectiveness, and failure to face problems. He said they ought to be ashamed of themselves; I replied that we should openly address ourselves to mistakes on both sides, and not gloss anything over.

Anyone who has any idea of the fertility of the land in Zambia and elsewhere – 'You could drive a walking stick into the ground and it would put out leaves,' was my own comment after a pleasant visit to Kenneth Kaunda – will find it hard to understand why six times as much grain has to be imported in the Eighties as in the early days of independence. Why did Zaïre, still an exporter of food in 1960, have to become dependent on food imports? Why must Liberia import rice it could grow for itself? (And in this respect the situation in the North African Maghreb area has not improved but deteriorated.)

The root of the evil usually lies in the fact that agriculture has become a poor relation, politically speaking. Food prices are held down to relieve the burden on the urban population. Governments cash in on agrarian exports. Farmers, on the other hand, get hardly any incentive to increase production. So the country becomes more and more dependent on imports, either bought or donated.

Emergency aid is necessary, but is no way to solve the problem. The unconventional Karlheinz Böhm, well-known actor and

self-made development activist in Ethiopia, is right to remind us
of the Chinese proverb which says, 'It is better to light a candle
than complain of the dark'. I support all readiness to give
humanitarian aid and every concrete project that will promote
self-help – an example being friends in Bavaria who have
'adopted' two villages suffering from drought in Mali. But wil-
lingly as support may be offered, we should not forget that
fundamental reforms are called for.

I am very much in favour of aid for Africa from the rest of the
world, especially Europe. But we must be clear about three
things:

- Except in genuine emergencies, it is irrational, because too
  expensive, to send highly subsidized foodstuffs to the developing countries instead of aiming for more effective results at less
  expense on the spot.
- Transport costs are often so high that they can hardly be
  justified – except, again, for emergency aid in disasters; funds
  should be invested in storage facilities on the spot.
- Something that is often entirely overlooked – by exporting our
  food, we are helping to introduce many of the developing
  countries to a form of nutrition that is not just expensive but
  wrong, and in addition to other things this is an injudicious
  import.

A good part of Europe's record grain harvest of 1984 went to
increasing aid early in 1985. I can only welcome that, the more so
as further aid in the way of encouraging self-help was planned.
Large parts of Africa have become accustomed to eating wheat,
which is not generally grown there. In West Africa, traditional
foods such as millet have been displaced by rice, which also comes
from abroad, and is either bought or donated. (Much money has
been spent on rice fields by the Niger, but the people of the Sahel
seem to have difficulty learning how to grow it.) To take another
example: if we send milk from Europe to Africa, it finds its way
into stomachs that are not used to it. And milk powder mixed
with tainted water does harm, not good.

Another reason why food imports are not the long-term way to
deal with the situation is that they offer no incentive to African

farmers, but, rather, discourage them. What is required is technical assistance, above all for the indigenous agriculture, and tools and committed experts, particularly to help cooperative institutions. Action must be taken against the disregard and neglect of the agricultural sector, and the fixing of agricultural producer prices which discourage production.

The 'green revolution' of the Sixties and Seventies, which achieved much in Pakistan, Sri Lanka, the Philippines and Indonesia as well as India, passed Africa by. But important results are expected from research at institutes in Nigeria (Ibadan), Kenya (Nairobi) and several other countries. The question remains: how seriously do we intend, over the years ahead, to encourage self-help in Africa and how much are we prepared to stand by the Africans if they are to bear the brunt of global political differences and of rearguard colonialist acts?

5. *Reform!*

Since the autumn of 1984 the World Bank has been trying to raise an additional $2 billion to relieve poverty in Africa. The programme had to be trimmed by half because of the recent US preference for avoiding multilateral arrangements, as they managed to do in this instance, thus setting the tone for others. (Though the United States gave, bilaterally, additional funds on its own account.)

One could not but feel doubtful of the policies of those governments in America and Europe which were now ready to help in the face of obvious famine, but had in the past either cut or discontinued their development aid – for instance, in Ethiopia. The US government rejected 50 credit proposals made on behalf of Africa by the World Bank and other institutions, among them six projects which were to have been to Ethiopia's advantage in 1984.

However, it was not and is not a matter of foreign financial aid alone; reform on the spot should be our chief concern. In many quarters there is still an aversion, ranging from incomprehension to hostility, to land reform and cooperatives. The subject thus tends to fare badly in resolutions which need unanimous support at government level. And favourable mention in a resolution does not necessarily mean that something will be done.

Internationally, agricultural production is coming to be valued more than it was only ten years ago. None the less, without fundamental changes there will be even worse shortages in even larger areas of the world over the next decade, particularly in Africa. Food aid can only alleviate, temporarily; it cannot solve the problem. It can be solved only by overcoming obsolete structures and ideologies, by actively including producers in their countries' policies, and by using the advances offered and promised us by science. And of course no progress can be made without capable administration.

There are now some countries in Asia and Latin America which show a relatively high growth rate in food production, and have become successful exporters, yet whose societies have large, poverty-stricken sections which are still inadequately provided for and undernourished. The food problem of such countries arises primarily from the fact that their people are too poor to buy what they need. It must be solved in the longer term by an improvement in income – which means providing remunerative jobs – for the members of these poor sections of society. That cannot be done without an economic policy which deliberately sets out to give revenues to those who need them.

Another group of countries is suffering chiefly (as seen in Africa) from the weakness of its agricultural production, poverty again being a factor, but the heart of their problem lies in the rapid decline in food production per head of the population. It is becoming prohibitively expensive to close this gap with imports. Environmental disasters and the destructive consequences of armed conflict add to these structural problems. But, first and foremost, in most of the countries with which we are concerned here, all progress made in food production is racing against population growth.

The already precarious situation became even more acute in the transition to the Eighties because of the devastating consequences of high oil prices in most Third World countries. More favourable prices or terms of payment, such as were granted to some of the poor countries by Latin American and Arab oil states, were not on the whole of any significance. The general situation was one in which, despite all economy measures, the oil bill consumed several times as large a share of export earnings as it had a few years earlier. Even in my Commission's report, we saw then 'no clear danger of a worldwide shortage of fertilizers', since only two or three per cent of oil production would be used for fertilizers. Nor was our observation wrong; it was just that prices rose sharply.

There was also another way in which the oil bill threatened food production. In many countries, people veered sharply to the use of wood as a fuel, with a consequent increase in wasteful exploitation and exhaustion of the land. Other alternatives, such as making petrol substitutes from sugar-cane, are highly controversial, since they do incalculable ecological damage, and decrease food production. What is needed is a programme to ensure world nutrition, based on the experience of recent years.

The *first* part of such a programme should be a purposeful increase in production. The main targets should be those countries with low incomes which show a deficit in their own production of foodstuffs. The increase could be achieved by price incentives and easier credit terms, and in many cases this could hardly be done without outside help. By increasing aid from abroad, an increase in agricultural investment at home could thus be encouraged. The least developed countries should be the chief focus of attention.

National and international *research* should concentrate, as much as they can, on the development of new, simple technologies suited to agriculture in tropical countries. They should be accompanied by programmes of joint study and organization. The developing countries themselves, with the support of their partner countries, would develop plans and programmes to deal with problems of marketing, transport and storage, and face the task, unfamiliar to their traditional agriculture, of supplying towns with food and opening up domestic markets.

Secondly, a supply of food from international sources must be secured. There should be a guarantee that at times of crisis, developing countries, particularly those agriculturally most at risk, could get supplies *in time*. However, the ultimate objective must be to strengthen those countries economically, to the point where they can supply themselves, in the world market if need be. Food aid for low-income countries should be stepped up appropriately; part of it (at least 20 per cent?) should be at the disposal of the United Nations' World Food Programme. Emergency reserves, as provided for by the International Wheat Agreement, should be stockpiled. Greater investment in storage capacity for the developing countries is needed too. Experts think that $1,000 million a year needs to be raised to create the necessary capacity on the spot *and* in the industrial countries.

Thirdly, we should look at international trade. For one thing, the producing countries should, at last, get adequate prices for their products. For another, tariff barriers should be lowered; one reason, but not the only one, is that it would then be easier for developing countries to increase their sales. In the course of the Seventies and the first half of the Eighties, trade in foodstuffs has made little contribution to economic growth in the developing countries.

Equal demands are made on the industrial and the developing countries. In the countries of the North, the attention of governments, of the public, and not least of influential economic circles, still needs to be directed to the urgent problems of the world food situation. Over and above emergency aid, an increased transfer of scientific and technical knowledge to the developing countries should be encouraged, particularly for the benefit of the great mass of the rural population. The countries of the South are confronted with the challenge to increase the value they set on their own agriculture. This would also mean letting the peasant population take a greater part in the decisions that affect them.

In 1984, the World Food Council came to the conclusion that over a 15-year period, $4 billion a year should be given for productive purposes and income support, in order to give 500 million people access to food by the end of the century. (My Commission set the figure at $4 billion a year over 20 years. It will be seen that the estimates are very close. Their ratio to arms spending is still horrific.)

The World Food Council was set up on the occasion of the World Food Conference at the end of 1974, when the famines immediately preceding it were fresh in people's minds. Two years later, the International Fund for Agricultural Development

(IFAD) was created, to boost agrarian production and food supplies with field projects, particularly in the poorest countries. The notable feature of this institution was the much increased participation and co-responsibility of the oil states. Western industrial countries, OPEC states and developing countries each had one third of the votes on its governing body, while finance ($1 billion in 1978–80) was originally divided between the industrial countries and the oil states. At the end of 1984 the activities of IFAD seemed to be under considerable threat, since the United States administration – in this as elsewhere – was anxious to take less part in international organizations (or multilateral agreements), placing more emphasis on bilateralism. Iran had stopped paying its contribution. Japan was also obstructing agreement, although this very fund had been seen as an excellent tool.

FAO, as the United Nations' special organization for food and agriculture, has not so far been affected. It has become the forum of worldwide discussion on agrarian policy; it also serves to coordinate concern about such questions as agrarian and nutritional planning, crop protection and the prevention of livestock epidemics. FAO has seen thousands of useful technical aid projects through. However, its headquarters in Rome has not escaped criticism. Even more than other international organizations, it has been accused of spending an increasing proportion of its budget on its own bureaucracy. Many of its critics, however, fail to make any comparisons with the growth of wages and salaries in their own national bureaucracies (or those of the European Community).

6. One Doctor for Tens of Thousands?

WHO, the United Nations' World Health Organization, which has its headquarters in Geneva, has stated its ambitious aim of making 'health for all' possible by the year 2000. WHO does not mean by this that it can eradicate all kinds of disease by then, but that it hopes to spread basic medical care and hygienic living conditions to all countries.

Dr Halfdan Mahler, the Danish Director-General of WHO, and his colleagues, strongly recommend concentration on basic care, with the provision of expensive equipment coming second. Most national health systems, they say regretfully in Geneva, cannot make good use of scientific and technical advances and achieve optimal effects in the face of their limited financial means.

However, we should cherish no illusions about the necessary expenditure. If the health strategy *agreed* upon in the context of WHO were put into practice, an additional $50 billion a year would be needed in the developing countries, i.e. rather more than the whole of present official development assistance. That seems beyond the limits of what we may now suppose feasible. Here again, however, it does no harm to remember the $1,000 billion a year which the human race thinks it can afford for military purposes.

Latest findings suggest that revolutionary results could be achieved in the battle against infant moratlity, in return for a relatively modest investment. Experts cooperating with UNICEF, on whose authority I am relying here, give cogent reasons to show that a cheap and simple 'mix' of sugar, salt and water could save 20,000 children a day. (Seen in terms of a year's mortality figures, the lives saved would be equivalent to the entire number of children under five growing up in Great Britain, West Germany, France, Italy and Spain.)

The 'mix', also known as ORT (Oral Rehydration Therapy), is to counteract diarrhoea, which is a great threat to small children. Other elements in the coming 'revolution' are:

- an effective programme of immunization, for instance against measles, TB and tetanus;
- propaganda to encourage breast-feeding;
- simple measuring charts which would tell mothers if their children were failing to grow properly;
- the provision of food supplements where a proper diet is otherwise unobtainable.

For the rest, no effective war can be waged against hunger if conditions of hygiene are not taken into account. High child mortality, particularly in the developing countries, can be overcome only if we understand that we are dealing with a combination of different adverse factors.

71

In many places, lack of clean water is easily the highest health risk. Lack of drinking water, altogether, has become more and more of a problem; supplies are uncertain in half the world. The Nepalese friend I quoted in the early pages of this book said, of certain hospitals that he knew, that if there had been clean water available locally, 80 per cent of their patients would never have come into hospital at all.

Encouraging progress in the processing of water can certainly be recorded in more than one part of the Third World. And there has been considerable success in the fight against epidemics as well: smallpox was virtually eradicated in the Seventies – a triumph for the World Health Organization and the countries concerned; cholera and malaria were brought under control in the Sixties.

Since then, they have spread again, because of lack of funds. From a report made by German doctors bringing emergency aid to Ethiopia: 'We see every imaginable kind of disease. Malaria is rife. So is typhus, so is amoebic dysentery, so are a great many eye diseases of all kinds. . . .'

There is a very great deal to be done, if one looks at statistics like these:

- Only 10 per cent of children in the developing countries are immunized against the six major childhood illnesses.
- 600 million people live in areas infested by parasites; they risk disease carried by flatworms which live in the blood vessels of the abdominal cavity (bilharziasis – the disease is so called after a German physician Bilharz).
- 300 million people suffer from parasitic worms.
- 100 million a year suffer from intestinal and respiratory diseases.
- Expectation of life has indeed risen, even in the Third World, but is still not much above 40 in a number of countries.
- In 1984, the USA had one doctor to 520 people, the Federal Republic of Germany had one to 450, but in Indonesia the ratio was one to 11,500, in Mali one to 32,000, and in Ethiopia one doctor to 58,000 people.

There is no automatic correspondence, however, between the average standard of living and health standards in different countries. Thus China and Sri Lanka may be extremely low-income countries, but they have an elementary health service for almost the whole of their populations. In Latin America, states as different as Costa Rica and Cuba lead the way in caring for the health of their citizens.

Politicians who are concerned with health and recognize their share of responsibility for the people of the Third World have begun to look at the problem of pharmaceutical drugs. This is all the more necessary as the avalanche of pills comes down on the developing countries too. Most of the products of the pharmaceutical industry used in those countries come from abroad. Quality and price are by no means always all they should be; one and the same drug often sells under different names and at different prices, according to the manufacturer's marketing power. Even worse: drugs which have been banned in industrial countries because of their dangers (for instance, because they are carcinogenic) are still being sold in the Third World.

Director-General Mahler of WHO has raised his voice in support of 'essential' medicaments: 'We have not yet been able to disentangle the complex relations between governments, national and international pharmaceutical industries, the medical profession and other professions in the public health services.' A statement which need not be taken as one of resignation.

7. Worldwide Assaults on the Environment

Concern for the health of those who live after us led me to the subject of environmental protection a quarter of a century ago. Members of the World Commission on Environment and Development established in 1984 were able to deliberate from a basis of extensive insights into their subject. They could assume that mutual dependency, to be observed at national, regional and international levels, exists between the economy, the environment, security and development. This Commission, which unlike mine or Olof Palme's arose from a resolution of the UN General

Assembly, works under the chairmanship of Gro Harlem Brundt-land, leader of the Norwegian Labour Party.

Worldwide assaults on our natural environment went un-noticed for a long time. So too did the additional interdependency which now links the industrial and developing countries through their ecological problems. Only five years ago, when the report of my Commission was published, there were many people who preferred to ignore what we had to say, over and above matters of international economic and humanitarian concern, on the sub-jects of the arms race *and ecology*. We spoke out on the growing risk to 'international common property', a risk arising from:

- deforestation and impoverishment of the soil,
- exhaustion of pastureland,
- depletion of fish stocks,
- air and water pollution.

If it took so long, and was so difficult, to get clear facts and the risks they entail into the minds of people in the industrial coun-tries, how can anyone be surprised to find the subject is con-sidered even less relevant in large parts of the developing coun-tries? A few years ago, in conversation with colleagues from developing countries, one had the impression that they thought ecology a Western luxury, and environmental protection a fanci-ful interest of culturally-minded tourists and big-game hunters. By now no one can fail to see that forests and water reserves are being depleted, while the deserts extend and nature is poisoned. Nor can anyone deny the consequences.

The poison gas disaster at the end of 1984 in the Indian city of Bhopal, which left 2,500 dead and over 100,000 injured, demon-strated the absurdity of the thesis that the protection of labour and the environment is only 'for rich countries, who can afford it'. On the contrary: attention was drawn to the fact that safety standards in the developing countries – as in that American pesticide factory in India – are set very considerably lower and applied far less stringently than in the countries where the tech-nologies concerned originated. (In Bhopal, it was impossible, even months later, to predict the consequences for those babies whose mothers had been in contact with the poison gas.)

The poison gas case, the death of forests, the contamination of foodstuffs are all connected on a major scale. Is it true, one may ask, that mankind has loosed destructive powers whose final effect will be the suicide of our species? Is it true that something is going on not unlike the behaviour of lemmings? I would like not to believe the comparison apt, but it is not surprising that a sense of hopelessness is spreading.

There can now be no serious argument – as was possible only a few years ago – against the proposition that natural resources are not inexhaustible. But even today, many will not admit to themselves that if we continue to exploit certain natural resources, notably coal and oil, as they have been exploited hitherto, they will last for only another half-century.

Issues of the natural resources and the environment caused the United Nations to hold a special conference in Stockholm in 1972. It led to the setting up of UNEP (the United Nations Environment Programme), an environmental organization with its headquarters in Nairobi. Only recently, under the leadership of this organization, several governments have declared it their minimum aim to reduce the release of pollutants into the environment by 30 per cent by the year 1993. . . .

Together with UNCTAD, the United Nations Conference on Trade and Development with its Secretariat in Geneva, UNEP has particularly recommended the governments of those developing countries rich in resources to introduce an effective environmental policy. Environmental considerations should play a greater part in the processing of primary commodities. Appropriate programmes could be financed by taxing output or export.

Not *everything* has been negative and disappointing over the last ten years. Rivers and lakes have been cleared of severe pollution, and have come back to life. Reafforestation has proved successful. It has been realized, if rather late in the day, that pollutant phenomena such as 'acid rain' could assume continental, even global proportions. And it had been widely hoped that the developing countries need not repeat all the same mistakes the industrial world had made.

In the course of the Seventies it became obvious that large parts of the Indian subcontinent, of sub-Saharan Africa, Central America and the Caribbean, and the South American Andes area are in great ecological danger. Destruction of the natural environment is the cause of periodic flooding in extensive regions of Asia.

If forests die, the entire vegetable kingdom is in mortal danger. Water and air and their degree of pollution depend on the forests to a great extent.

- Since 1960, FAO estimates that the world has lost half its forests.
- Every year forests all over the world shrink by a further several million hectares.
- The deforestation of large areas of tropical rain forest in Latin America (especially the Amazon basin), Africa and South-east Asia has far-reaching climatic consequences, going beyond the particular regions concerned; they are an encumbrance to agriculture.
- By the end of the century, the supply of usable wood will be considerably reduced; hundreds of millions of people will have lost their traditional fuel for cooking.
- Soil erosion, which has occurred on a large scale in, for instance, the Himalayas, is regarded as a direct consequence of deforestation and unsuitable hydraulic construction works.
- Some governments of developing countries themselves saw the problem earlier than most, and (as in East Africa) appealed to their people: 'Help your environment, and your environment will help you.'
- Years ago, in Tunisia and Kenya and later in India and China, I saw what efforts were being made to grow new forests; there are reports of similar efforts in Korea. (I shall come to Cuba and Israel later.)

In the field of *energy*, a start has been made on making a 'transition . . . from high dependence on increasingly scarce non-renewable energy sources', as we put it in the first report of my Commission. Economic use of energy can be perceived in many quarters, and the deceleration of economic growth makes an involuntary contribution. The cartel of oil-exporting countries no longer strikes terror into us as it did a decade ago. The transition to inexhaustible energy sources has begun: solar energy in the widest sense, use of the biomass, the wind and the tides.

I remember, only a few years ago, the arrogant smiles of those government officials who could make nothing of reports about simple pumps powered by solar cells (for instance, to generate power for the lighting of a hospital at Bamako [Mali] and its operating theatre). Converting the rays of the sun, which in the tropics have until now rather been a draw on human strength, into a large source of cheap energy has become a major concern of our time.

The work necessary to make solar technology an economic proposition is in progress. I am told by experts that it will be only another few decades before solar power stations can be put into space to convert energy. (There is still controversy as to whether we can make the transition from the age of oil to the age of alternative energy sources successfully without increased reliance on nuclear energy; it may depend upon whether we can command *new* forms of energy.)

The USA did not accept our proposal for the creation of a global energy research centre under United Nations auspices and affiliated to the World Bank, to help in opening up new energy sources in the poorest countries. Intensive exploration into mineral resources in the Third World calls for such backing, since poor countries simply cannot raise the funds and should not be subject to unfair agreements. (There are huge reserves of hydro power in Africa which might be utilized.)

At the end of 1984 a private research institute in the United States warned that further waste of *water reserves* would lead in the next decade to a global crisis comparable to the oil crisis. At almost the same time, a Harvard University institute stated that *no* worldwide water shortage need be feared until well into the next century. But it entered a caveat: regionally, for instance in West Africa, a serious dearth of supplies must be expected. According to UN estimates, half of all the people of the Third World are today without fresh drinking water. Their number increases by 20 million annually.

The endangering of water reserves by over-use, excessive pumping of groundwater and its increasing degree of contamination has become a major political concern. In the summer of

1984, the Executive Director of UNEP,* Mostafa K. Tolba, said at a seminar in Japan that the growing scarcity of drinking water would aggravate international economic and political problems, impairing the security of many states.

We became really sensitive to the price of oil only when the oil states made it expensive. We still act as if water cost nothing, whereas in fact it can be as expensive as oil. In tomorrow's industrial society careful and thus sparing use of natural resources will have to be taken as much for granted as it is now (or should be) taken for granted that labour and capital will be employed as economically as possible in a business venture. One of the more cheering phenomena of a generally unpleasant international perspective is the fact that the superpowers have stated their intention of upholding the agreement which came into force in 1978, banning 'environmental changes for hostile purposes'. We should also welcome the fact that environmentalist objectives which would husband resources are beginning to take effect on economic cooperation, in sharp contrast to the state of affairs only a few years ago, and that demands are even sometimes made for them to be given equal status with the traditional areas of negotiation in foreign politics.

In 1972 the bad news emanating from the Club of Rome was widely considered much dramatized, more of a fanciful picture of the future than anything else. Not only do those in positions of political responsibility now know better; what is known is taken more seriously than a decade ago. Ordinary people are better informed, and expect political action to follow on the heels of knowledge. Majorities are beginning to realize that the protection of our living conditions is just as valuable as a modern economy which is technically up to date and which makes no more demands on people than is necessary. Humane labour, effective protection of the environment and an environmentally conscious management of the economy must complement each other and the safeguarding of peace.

* UNEP should not be confused with UNDP. The latter is the – technical – United Nations Development Programme, directed over a number of years by the energetic Bradford Morse, a former American Congressman who is now in charge of the World Bank's special programme for Africa.

IV

THE POPE AND THE 'DIMENSION OF EVIL'

In the summer of 1978 I visited Rome as chairman of my Commission. Pope Paul VI, who obviously had little time left to him, set out his view that 'development is another word for peace', saying that in his opinion the social issue had assumed global proportions.

On my visits to Geneva, I met Philip Potter, then General Secretary of the World Council of Churches, which emphatically believed that peace is not simply the absence of war and that, 'Peace cannot be built on unjust foundations'.

In Germany I had a friendly reception from our two largest religious groups, the Catholic and the Protestant Churches, and other religious communions. The Pope, in moving terms, adjured us to continue our self-imposed task. The Commission, he said, represented 'hope for us and for the progress of the nations'.

At my meeting with Cardinal Arns in São Paulo, I sensed great understanding and encouragement. I must not enter into the theological side of the debate on liberation theology, but I was deeply impressed to find the clergy, particularly in Latin America, ranging themselves so unequivocally on the side of the poor and weak. The same applies to the earnest concern with which the bishops of North America present their joint pastoral message of an 'option for the poor', logically applying that message also to questions of international economic and trade relations. If such ideas are formulated within the Church of the richest country on earth, it may be an indication that the challenge of the South is to some extent beginning to be felt in Northern industrial states.

The commitment of the Church achieves much in the Third World; no criticism of outdated or unworldly attitudes – as in the area of family planning and birth control – can alter that. In West Germany, the churches have contributed in no small measure to arousing and deepening an understanding of the problems of developing countries. Their relief organizations and projects, like other non-government organizations, have helped to establish direct contact between the donors and recipients of development aid. They are aware that their efforts can be no substitute for what governments leave undone. No commitment on the part of the Church can compensate for exorbitant interest rates, or under-payment for raw materials, or state-imposed controls on imports from developing countries. But it is greatly to be hoped that the churches will not slacken their own efforts. Their work encourages the practical understanding of interconnections and circumstances which ought to be borne in mind when political and economic decisions are taken. And at that point too the churches should keep urging those in positions of political responsibility to do their part.

When I speak with prominent representatives of the Church, particularly the younger ones, and we explore the causes leading to violent conflict and war, our talk is not just of ideological confrontation and human rights, but is increasingly concerned with:

- high levels of armaments,
- injustices within the world economy, and
- the increasing hunger and need still suffered by so many.

Olof Palme and his Commission, and I and my own colleagues, were in Rome together at the beginning of 1984, at the invitation of our friend Bettino Craxi, the Italian Premier. Pope John Paul II received us. I told him we were not the kind of people who would ask how many divisions of soldiers the Pope had at his disposal: 'Hope is an important element in overcoming obstacles which might otherwise seem insuperable ... all who believe in the power of sincere convictions should reach out their hands to each other.' Our vision, I added, was of an international order in which the possession of nuclear weapons would not be the deciding factor in world politics, and security could be maintained at a much lower level, while material potential was used for the good of the peoples.

The Pope, for his part, reminded us that he had often referred to the links between those two great complex issues of North–South and East–West relations: 'The challenges and problems facing humanity everywhere now transcend national and regional boundaries. . . . If the social issue has today assumed global proportions, then the concrete programmes adopted by nations and regions must spring from a full awareness of that fact, and they must try from the first to assess the consequences such projects will have for the peoples and nations directly or indirectly affected.' Humanity, he said, will never let itself be reduced to a mere object or a one-dimensional factor.

In the autumn of 1984 the Pope described the great gulf between North and South as 'a universal dimension of injustice and evil'. A German cardinal was equally unequivocal when he added, a little later, that to arm ourselves for war was theft, 'since it takes the bread out of the mouths of the poor'.

I suggested earlier that peace may be seen as the objective or wish of all religions, forms of belief and basic philosophical attitudes. Should it not be possible, I ask once more, to deduce from this a *common* desire for peace, and draw from it the emotional and moral incentive to make fresh efforts? I added then that this was another point on which one should cherish no illusions: the creation of order out of contradictions seems to be humanity's eternal task. The momentum provided by the churches and religious communions *can* strengthen global solidarity and contribute to the solution of North–South problems.

V

WHAT SHOULD BE CHANGED?

1. *Straight Talk*

What are the main tasks which face us in the area of North–South relations? There is still not enough clarity on this point.

First, we must understand that there is now a worldwide interconnection of effects. We speak of interdependency, or the globalization of interaction – the interaction of population growth, economic development, the use of commodities and energy, all bound up with rapid and accelerating technical developments. On the other hand, political capabilities and an understanding of international responsibility seem to be stagnating. There are clear signs of a retrogressive movement in many areas. In the struggle against unemployment, there is not a clear enough distinction between what can be done nationally and what must be attempted at a European or international level. As for environmental problems, international connections are coming to be recognized, if only gradually. But we are still slow to recognize that the question of our future-oriented realization of our own interests arises in our relation with the poorer sections of humanity.

Secondly, the ideological differences between powers and power blocs can no longer be resolved by violent conflict. That is ruled out once and for all by the very real danger, a danger of an entirely new kind, that we might mutually destroy each other – all of us, in the North and the South, the East and the West. Out of that comes the new realization that henceforth we can achieve security only together, *with* each other. What used to be a matter of goodwill is now an inescapable necessity.

Thirdly – and this surely is even harder – we must examine our own way of life, our ideas and what we believe to be our aims, and face the fact that poverty, ignorance and disease make large numbers of men and women the slaves of their circumstances. As long as those evils that could be overcome with more of an effort still spread, we must go on reminding ourselves that in the long run such a situation cannot last.

It can be seen without too much difficulty that these three main questions are very closely connected. This is particularly clear if once again we look squarely at the most important consequence of lack of undertanding of the interconnections – the senseless proliferation of weapons of destruction.

The ability of the generation now coming to the age of responsibility to solve the problems I have mentioned will decide how humanity copes with the transition to a new kind of global equilibrium. One may assume that urgently needed investments can be made only when a considerable part of our present resources is diverted to productive uses.

And considerable investments are indeed needed if a transition is to be made to a reasonably stable world with a population of ten or even fifteen billion in the next century. We know that the developing countries cannot raise the funds they need through domestic savings. But this problem *can* be solved. In principle, the resources required *can* be made available. Humanity *is* capable of solving the problem of finding those resources.

Quite another matter is whether we shall succeed in overcoming both the current lack of understanding of the interconnections, and the superfluity of special interests, in time. To succeed there must be much greater cooperation, both between specialists and generalists, particularly in development planning but in many other areas too. What we lack at the moment is an adequate link between expert knowledge and a contextual understanding. The present tendency is to undertake complex projects on the basis of simplistic assumptions, with the result that aims are only rarely achieved, while side effects which had not been envisaged further prejudice the outcome.

It is not easy to avoid such blind alleys. We should do well to forgo dogmatic trifling and speak clearly and to the point. This much seems obvious: it is only through greater global solidarity, through the pluralistic coexistence of differing principles, and through a greater ability to see the context, that we shall create a world in which many, and if possible all, will have their share of common welfare and justice. International cooperation in a spirit of courage and imagination can help to overcome the international crisis.

There is no sense in dogmatic disputes about free markets or central planning. Still less so when keen advocates of the free market economy sanction state intervention to benefit endangered branches of industry – dockyards here, steelworks there, this branch of industry today and perhaps that one tomorrow – while conversely the central planners in the East call for more personal initiative and introduce their own kind of market strategies. When Americans and Europeans alike have expensive market regulations for their own agricultural products, just as the industrial countries of the East do in some other fields, we ought not to reject corresponding demands made by the developing countries in the matter of commodities until we can say our own conduct is right and reasonable.

There is much argument as to whether the economy should be left to itself, or within what framework it should operate. The answer by no means decides *which* kind of economy and in particular what kind of price formation is preferable. Confusion reigns on these points. Whether a country inclines rather more to a market economy or to state control need not concern us. We have become used to seeing both coexist in our countries; why should they not coexist elsewhere too?

The sound of arrogant ideologists blowing their own trumpets is no less irritating than the self-satisfied air of those who regard themselves as realistic politicians, or the self-important gabbling of bureaucrats holding forth about concern for humanity. But the time bomb is ticking away, and despair is no help.

2. Not All in the South Are Poor

Political relations between the various parts of the world have changed fundamentally since the end of the Second World War. A system built up over a period of more than 300 years collapsed within 25. First India, Indonesia and – in a different way – China, then the former English, French and Belgian colonies of Africa, and finally the former Portuguese colonies, all became politically independent; viceroys or governors or whatever they might be called went back to Europe. (The Germans were a special case, last out and first home again, having lost their colonies along with the First World War.)

Or is this view of matters wrong, at least when put that way? Is it too Eurocentric? Mention should at least be made of the Japanese, who ruled 450 million people in Asia around 1942, and were then thrown back on their native islands (losing some areas of those as well). And nothing can now be understood in isolation from the role of the two superpowers that emerged from the Second World War.

Of the 159 member states of the United Nations (in 1984) the numbers divided up into:

- 127 developing countries,
- 20 Western industrial countries,
- 12 countries with planned economies (of which China and Cuba are also classed as developing countries).

In some UN organizations, the following classification has been in use for some time:

- A: African and Asian developing countries,
- B: Western industrial countries,
- C: Latin American developing countries,
- D: Eastern planned-economy countries,
- China to a certain extent forms a group on its own.

A designation for the developing countries more generally used is the 'Group of 77', actually numbering 126 states at the end of 1984. This 'group' was formed in 1964, when UNCTAD (the United Nations Conference on Trade and Development) was first convened.

The oversimplified classification of countries into groups does not do justice to the complex reality. It is easy to distinguish between former colonies and their former colonial rulers – but a distinction between North and South, if by that we mean to distinguish between rich and poor countries, can be drawn only if one adds some clarifications. In any case, the world is not so constituted that the North can be described outright as 'rich' and the South as 'poor'. Even apart from other differences, we all know that not everyone in the North is rich, nor everyone in the South poor.

'North', at the risk of simplification, stands for the 'old' industrial countries, not just for the West; 'South', at a similar risk of misleading simplification, stands for all the countries whose economic development has been retarded not exclusively, but largely, by colonialism.

> The North–South split expressed in figures:
> - Just under a third of the world's population lives in the North, with over four-fifths of the world's income at its disposal.
> - Among the 'rich' countries, those with 'market economies' are far in advance of those with 'planned economies'.
> - Of the poor countries, those with 'market economies' get a share of 12 per cent of world revenue, and the 'planned economy' countries of Asia (in particular China!) get 5 per cent. The gross national product per head of the population in most developing countries is between $150 and $1,500 a year.

Income per head and the share of the poor countries in world revenue are generally put even lower in statistics than they are in fact, since the barter economy and dealings in kind are hard to record statistically.

The make-up of the world by states offers a confused picture, and current concepts are not entirely suited to clarifying it:

- The 'North', as well as taking in North America, Japan, the European West and the Soviet Union with her European allies, is also understood to include two rich industrial countries south of the Equator, Australia and New Zealand.

- In Asia, Japan counts as part of the 'West', and so again do Australia and New Zealand in the Pacific.
- Japan, more heavily dependent than Europe on the developing countries, where she makes a very large part of her direct investments, rose to become the second strongest economic power in the world within a generation.
- Countries regarded as belonging to the 'East' are the German Democratic Republic, Czechoslovakia and other Central European countries, Cuba in the Caribbean, and sometimes Ethiopia in Africa.
- A country like Mexico may lie in the North, but counts as part of the 'South'.
- There are countries located in the South, particularly among the oil-exporting Arab states of the Gulf, which have a higher *per capita* income than prosperous industrial countries.
- Not all countries such as Nigeria, Indonesia and Mexico are rich because they export oil.
- In the 'South', as in the 'North', there are instances of extreme differences in prosperity; some countries sell a great quantity of foodstuffs while many of their own people do not have enough to eat.
- Ireland, Greece, Portugal and Spain belong to the European Community (and to OECD, the Organization for Economic Cooperation and Development, with its headquarters in Paris, which grew out of the Marshall Plan); however, they are nowhere near as prosperous as the USA, or the Federal Republic of Germany, or Sweden.
- Romania sets store by being included among the developing countries, and in that respect is comparable to non-aligned Yugoslavia. Does that decrease Romania's association with Comecon?
- Does the fact that Hong Kong, Singapore, Kuwait and Bahrain belong to the 'Group of 77' make them poor?
- The ASEAN group – the Association of South-East Asian Nations, including Thailand, Malaysia, Indonesia, Singapore, the Philippines, and latterly also Brunei – has a good chance of healthy development with considerable annual growth.
- Finally, it is surely confusing to lump together countries which have an old-established industrial base such as Argentina,

Brazil, Mexico, and Colombia and Venezuela, or aspiring countries such as South Korea, Taiwan and Malaysia, with the poverty-stricken regions of the Sahel zone, Bangladesh or Haiti.

And another thing to be remembered is that not everything which succeeds in Kenya will necessarily succeed in India. An Eastern European head of state did not hesitate to tell me one of his anxieties: it is one thing, he said, to build a factory in the Mongolian People's Republic, another to rely on its being efficiently run thereafter.

Not only in South-East Asia but in some Latin American countries too, industrial development has been erratic. The twenty countries which had the fastest growth in the Seventies were all Third World countries, and some of them stand on the brink of full industrialization. (Argentina, Brazil, Chile, Mexico and Uruguay are regarded as newly industrializing countries; so are Hong Kong, Singapore, South Korea and Taiwan.) The old industrial states have now lost their pre-eminence in a whole range of industries, not only in such areas as textiles and shoes, but in steel, ship-building, railroad construction, mechanical engineering, and the manufacturing of parts for the market in photographic equipment, electronics and computers.

The 'bloc of poor countries', if it ever existed, has been eroded by a number of very different circumstances and interests. On one hand, we find the rich among the oil-producing countries, into which money is still pouring at a considerable if no longer exuberant rate; on the other, countries like Tanzania, Cambodia, Bolivia and Bangladesh; in between them, newly industrializing countries with their debt mountains, to which I shall return when considering the case of Latin America.

The collective term 'Third World', which appears frequently in this book, has become customary to describe the developing countries. The expression was coined in Paris at the beginning of the Fifties, and applied to those countries which, exploited and despised like the Third Estate before the French Revolution, now wanted to 'make something of themselves'. No one was ever quite sure what the First and Second Worlds were supposed to be. The Old World and the New World, or the Western World and the

Eastern World? In Mao's time, the Chinese Communists tried drawing their own kind of distinction: the two superpowers or 'hegemonists' were the First World, the Western Europeans and some countries in a comparable situation the Second World, with the Second regarded on the one hand as a participant in the oppression of the Third World, while on the other it might be won over as an ally against the 'hegemonists'. . . .

So far as the governments making up the group of developing countries, or the 'Group of 77', are concerned, it is not essentially different from the uncommitted or Non-aligned Countries Movement, which has grown from 25 to 104. At its founding conference in Belgrade in 1961 – there was an Afro–Asian forerunner in Bandung in 1955 – the question of peace and the problems of development were described as of equal importance. Nehru, Nasser and Tito formed a kind of executive committee, and right up to the time of his death in 1980 Tito opposed all attempts to bind the uncommitted countries to one of the superpowers. The 'movement' has no permanent secretariat. Unlike the 'Group of 77', it has no group status within the United Nations.

I had a chance to see Tito's firm commitment to East–West and North–South issues for myself in the summer of 1979, when I visited him for the last time on the island of Brioni. Tito played a considerable part in making the non-aligned countries into a factor which cannot be disregarded and at times is influential, and in reminding the Northern part of the world of its duties towards the South, as well as in reminding the great powers of their duty to maintain peace.

(The Commonwealth, with 49 member states, plus Namibia, stands rather outside the rest of the scheme; a loose grouping, it is the legacy of the British Empire, and has launched many useful initiatives over the years.)

The 'action programme for a new international economic order' upon which a summit conference of the non-aligned countries decided in Algiers in 1973, was the subject of talks I had a few months later with President Boumedienne of Algeria, and with President Echeverria, then President of Mexico, after a Special Session of the United Nations had adopted a 'Charter of Economic Rights and Duties of States'. What they were advocating seemed to me very schematic, not free of contradictions, and also excessively sure of the value of resolutions. In fact, they had more right on their side than their uncomprehending opponents, though they did not take the far-reaching objective differences between developing countries into account, let alone the differences within most of those countries. But it was to be only a decade before an EEC Commissioner, the former French Foreign Minister Claude Cheysson, was to say that the creation of a new international economic system was an even more decisive factor for world peace than the resolution of conflicts between the superpowers. The one is certainly no less important than the other.

3. *Whose Development?*

At the end of 1982, three years after the first report of my Commission, we said in our second report that 'the Commission foresaw the world community in the 1980s facing much greater dangers than at any time since the Second World War'. The prospects had now, we said, become even darker, with:

- the international recession, which could deepen into depression;
- massive unemployment in the countries of the North, and the threat of economic collapse in parts of the Third World;
- acute risk to the international financial system, and growing disorder in world trade;
- the renewed arms race, as well as wars and civil strife in numerous Third World countries.

Another few years have passed since then. In the USA and some (but far from all) industrial countries, a certain economic recovery has begun. But this is still problematical, and there are hints of fresh setbacks. We cannot yet discount the possibility that the Eighties will become a decade of disasters.

The great contrast between the satisfaction of needs in North and South, and destitution in the Third World, have spread yet further. Thus it is only too easy to see why people wonder whether many of the developing countries could not do more themselves to get the problems under control. Indeed, one quite often hears it asked whether 'they' are doing anything at all, or just relying too much, and unjustifiably, on outside help.

This argument, if it is one, concurs with the misleading thesis of that Oxford international economist who said that foreign aid inhibits instead of accelerating development. But the assumption that public development aid has done more harm than good in Third World countries is downright wrong. The fact that some ambitious projects have turned out to be of little relevance is quite another matter. There is no doubt that the developing countries and their financial backers have had to learn from such mistakes and were often slow to do so. And no one is claiming that no more mistakes will ever be made. But why overlook the large number of defective projects in industrial countries? Why should the criteria be set so much higher for the developing countries?

The arch-conservative Lord Bauer, a Hungarian by birth, but who has worked at the London School of Economics for a number of years, goes further: development aid, he says, encourages a dependent mentality, begets corruption and shores up incompetent governments; it is 'the cause and not the solution' of the North–South conflict. Moreover, in his view, the population explosion does not impede but encourages economic growth. Nor does he see mineral resources as a necessary precondition of growth – it depends entirely on the correct economic policy and the values on which it is founded. Professor Bauer is among the harshest critics of the World Bank and other international institutions.

My old friend Gunnar Myrdal, the Swedish political economist and Nobel Prize winner – a man of wide interests, as expressed in his great work on the race problem in the United States and a major book on Asia – has been associated with criticism of this kind; unjustly, but there is no doubt that he did perform a considerable volte-face. His main targets are the enrichment of élites and the incompetence of bureaucracies and he deplores the fact that much aid was thus wasted. We should tell the Third World, says Professor Myrdal, that the new economic order has to begin in their own countries. In practical terms, this means the donation of aid in times of disaster, while normal economic relations should be the rule for the rest of the time. . . .

As anyone will understand, I cannot myself adopt this line, which betrays great disillusion. But let us not hide the fact that similar ideas are sometimes voiced in the South itself. B. P. Koirala, whom I have already mentioned, thought that foreign aid did not advance the cause of development, but merely created a new class whose prosperity had nothing to do with the condition of the people. 'The new class is not economically rooted in its country. It exists solely on a basis of the manipulation of foreign aid by means of corruption and illegal trade.'

In a report on Nigeria I found the following: 'Corruption in the economy, the administration and the military will persist as long as the immediate "survival interests" of poorly paid civil servants or the exaggerated material need for luxury goods are latent in the middle and upper classes of society.'

Abuse of power is an evil in *all* parts of the world. At my request experts gave me the names of the countries which would be at the very top of any ranking in this respect. Extravagance and corruption, abuse of power, militarization for the purpose of maintaining power, may be found in many parts of the world, not just countries of the South. We can speak of a good example being set by the industrial countries only to a limited degree. An open dialogue between North and South must mean that no subject is excluded: not the pressure exerted by strong governments, nor fraudulent dealings on the part of powerful business concerns, nor the abuse of power by so-called élites. And if we go by the United Nations Charter, the destitution of refugees, the mistreatment of minorities, and infringement of the simplest human rights cannot be excluded from a claim on the common interest.

At the same time, we shall have to live with the fact that the claim to sovereignty of representatives of some young states will be made particularly forcefully – all the more so when they can plead an old culture. We must realize that reproving forefingers raised too often and too easily lead to 'us in the North' having the record of our own sins held against us. And among them are those sins we have exported. The one-sided apportioning of blame is no help. It is important to recognize our own as well as the general responsibility, both in the present and the future, and to understand that small states, and states of medium size, and states of fairly large size too, must find a common denominator between their own interests and those of others if they mean to hold their own to any extent.

As for what development is really supposed to mean, and whose development we are talking about – there is more than one answer to that question. At least we shall not start out as confidently as they did a generation ago from the assumption that the 'underdeveloped' countries should be developed to conform with the material standards of ourselves (or the Americans) and that the whole world would be well advised to imitate the model of the highly industrialized countries.

These days, there is justifiable doubt in more than one quarter as to whether development can simply be equated with growth of every kind. It is hard to imagine development without growth. But not every kind of growth leads to development, let alone progress. The question is rather: *what* do we want to see grow, and *how*, in order to encourage *whose* development? Even in our own latitudes, there is an increasing number of people who wonder if it can really be humanity's highest aim to live in crowded accommodation, consuming unnecessarily large amounts of energy and eating fast food. The developing countries should go their own way. Their peoples must be allowed to decide for themselves what kind of progress they want, and what elements of *their* cultural inheritance they wish to perpetuate. It cannot be any business of ours to press new (or old) models upon them, act as their guardians or take them under our wing. Anyone who recommends a mere process of 'catching up' to our own level misunderstands the facts, or his own sphere of responsibility.

The real aim of a country's development should lie in its self-fulfilment and ability to participate in creative partnership. Our Commission assumed that development was in any case more than a transition from poverty to wealth, from a traditional agrarian economy to urbanized, industrial ways of life. The concept of development, to those who think as we do, contains not only the notion of material prosperity, but also the idea of something more in the way of human dignity, security, justice and equality. For the rest, we said, we were not trying to redefine the now questionable concept of development. Our concern was not with the niceties of theoretical notions, but with the fact that so many people are living in almost inconceivable poverty, and that so much needs to be done to help ward off the worst of that misery.

Attempts to penetrate the problem through theory – and there are several variants from the Marxist viewpoint alone – deserve some attention, and I would just like to mention two points: First, the current theory that imperialism is the exploitation of the 'periphery' by the 'centre' need not in principle be at variance with our present survival interests, which transcend all systems. Secondly, alongside the failure of 'liberal' strategies of the catching-up variety is the fact that a considerable trade is growing between developing countries, or some of them.

It is beginning to be widely felt that we must free ourselves from any idea of the desirability of spoon-feeding others. The point is not what others should do, but what we are ready to do together with them. The fact that development begins at home is one of the important realizations of the last few years. Ways of life and methods of production which are not destructive need encouragement. In the process, it will not always be technical quality which matters, but a new spirit of solidarity, and of respect for the space in which individuals have freedom to act and for the common good.

Among those in positions of responsibility in the South there are quite a number who speak frankly about the weaknesses of their associations; the moral corruption that always proceeds from absolute power; the flight from responsibility; the 'naïve belief in rhetoric and the volume of noise' (Ramphal).

The problems facing the South, which were described in detail in my Commission's two reports, can in all essential respects be brought nearer a solution only by the people of the South themselves. It was our colleagues from the developing countries who put forward this proposition, and set it down on paper. The countries of the South as a whole, however, have no machinery that is at all suitable for an era of negotiations. It is a drawback that the developing countries have not managed to set up a joint secretariat. And this is a task which could hardly have been solved *for* them, unless by a decision to make the necessary modifications to UNCTAD, with the agreement of all member countries.

In the autumn of 1984, shortly before I went to Cartagena in Colombia, representatives of the Group of 77 meeting there endorsed their intention of introducing a system of mutually preferential trading, in order to extend the exchange of goods between themselves; three years earlier, an action programme had been decided upon in Caracas. Bringing about more economic cooperation *between* the developing countries was another important subject discussed at the conferences of the non-aligned countries. A certain amount of progress can now be recorded, and we may hope for something to come of the South–South dimension in international trade.

The prosperous oil states have not yet managed to summon up any enthusiasm for a 'Bank of the South'. During Latin America's severe debt crisis, much was heard there of a coordinated approach to creditors, but nothing much of a practical nature came of it outside conferences. However, there is no doubt that cooperation in regional areas looks like becoming a more important factor. It is not something that can be kept on ice until all possible ills have been done away with in the individual countries concerned.

The familiar inconsistencies of human behaviour hold good of North–South relations, among them the fact that people think they must compensate and indeed over-compensate for losses. Material interests are frequently given an ideological camouflage. Much proselytizing is done, and massive influence is brought to bear, under the banner of self-determination. Particularly in cultural respects, anything but liberalism and non-intervention is practised – instead, influence is exerted according to whatever the proponent of non-interventionism wants. Development aid and economic cooperation are often enough pursued as a continuation of an old state of affairs by new means. Quite a number of former colonial civil servants meet again in the employment of the World Bank, or working as experts in their old countries, but now in the service of a new ministry for economic cooperation or similar agency.

To call incompetence, social arrogance and injustice in the Third World by their right names means not sweeping anything under the carpet, yet not making ourselves out to be any better than we are. Justice did not prevail in our own states from the very first, and it is still something achieved only with difficulty. 'They' in the South did not inflict economic crises and world wars on 'us' in the North.

4. A New Bretton Woods?

At the Bretton Woods conference towards the end of the Second World War, agreements were made which, under the leadership of the United States, were to prove their worth to the international monetary system (and to policies of financial cooperation) for an amazingly long time. Today, there is not a country which, on its own, has that concentrated economic power and discipline in monetary policy which would be necessary to help the world to a sound system. International trade and the interdependence of the international economy have increased far more than any participant in that conference at Bretton Woods may ever have imagined. Economic power has spread into a wider area today, and mutual international dependence has to a great extent become reality. Yet confidence in international cooperation has been shaken, and indeed is largely lost.

At Bretton Woods – which was nothing but a railroad station and the address of a fine, pleasantly situated New Hampshire hotel – the Americans and British between them laid the foundations of the financial and monetary system which turned out to be functional in its own way for nearly three decades.

The Bretton Woods negotiations themselves were described as difficult, although the number of participants was modest compared with the 146 member states which now belong to the World Bank. But even then, in that smaller circle, it was hard to convince many of those taking part of the benefits of international agreements. Even the Americans initially had considerable reservations, although the new system was much to their advantage. Harry Dexter White, leading the American delegation, warned his fellow countrymen and his own government that if success depended on taking bold action and taking it swiftly, they could not afford protracted negotiations, and where all-embracing economic, political and social questions were concerned, small national advantages should give way. In his own words: 'We must substitute, before it is too late, imagination for tradition; generosity for shrewdness; understanding for bargaining; toughness for caution; and wisdom for prejudice. We are rich – we should use more of our wealth in the interest of peace.'

The 'East' took part in the negotiations but did not join the institutions decided upon at the Bretton Woods conference; the Soviet Union was not happy about the idea of transferring part of its gold holdings. Numerically, the 'South' was poorly represented, although India and several important Latin American countries participated. Naturally the 'enemy states', headed by Germany and Japan, were not invited to attend. Better adjusted participation of all interested parties is thus one of the subjects which should figure prominently in any discussion of the reform of the international institutions which were then established.

The Bretton Woods system was visibly shaken by the oil crisis of 1973/74, but it had already ceased to function well at the beginning of the Seventies. The convertibility of the dollar into gold was abandoned in 1971, when the United States could not bring itself to cover the cost of the Vietnam War by laying a greater burden on its own national economy. It had been financing its deficits for too long by putting more and more dollars into circulation. The result was a change of attitude towards the dollar. Exchange rates adjustments were expected, and international capital movements began. The sudden reversal of the flow of international payments as the result of the oil price crisis finished the job.

Only very slowly, particularly in the USA, did people begin to understand that these changes had much farther-reaching consequences, than what the long queues at petrol stations and the increased demand for smaller cars indicated. The people of the oil-exporting countries could not eat their billions, any more than they had previously been able to drink their oil. So to a great extent the money flowed back into the banks of the industrial countries, whether as direct investments or credits. 'Recycling', as it was called, was in fashion, and ostensibly it seemed to be a great success.

There was a similar picture after the second oil shock in 1979/80. The banks granted yet more credits, debts rose higher,

International institutions set up at Bretton Woods:

- The International Monetary Fund (IMF), to be the guardian of monetary order. It was to concern itself with stable exchange rates and liquidity to support free trade. Of recent years the debt crisis has altered and in some respects enhanced its role.

- The World Bank (officially IBRD, the International Bank for Reconstruction and Development). Its first task was opening up the way to reconstruction in Europe and Japan by means of loans. Later, its real work was to encourage the developing countries.

- Lord Keynes, the eminent British economist, wanted an International Trade Organization (ITO) set up at Bretton Woods as well, but the Havana Agreement, negotiated with this in mind, was not ratified by the United States Congress.

- The proposed ITO was also to have concerned itself with the stabilization of commodity prices. Had that suggestion been followed up, serious disagreements – and considerable damage to the developing countries – could have been avoided later.

- GATT, the General Agreement on Tariffs and Trade, was created as an indirect result of Bretton Woods. Its headquarters are in Geneva, and it now has 90 members. Originally intended only as a temporary arrangement, it turned into an important forum for multilateral talks on trade.

and no one felt too much concerned. But the flow of money was not quite so regular now. A huge so-called Eurodollar market (i.e. a market for dollars held outside the United States) had developed, the result of the circumstances in which some – the banks – were eager to invest their liquid funds, and others – not least the oil-importing developing countries – were equally eager to ask for new loans. The Eurodollar market grew from a few billion, originally intended only to balance payments at the margin and, as it were, keep the old system running, to a vast size, expanding to $1,000 billion or even $2,000 billion. For several years, and generally without any control by the central banks, money was moved from country to country, wherever there seemed to be the smallest danger of devaluation. Great fluctuations in exchange rates ensued, and entire economies veered off course. The end-product was high interest rates, for it had become increasingly necessary to halt inflation, and moreover the new sources of money were beginning to dry up.

Today one cannot overlook the fact that the world economy has been badly scarred. The scars stem from the fact that it was left to market forces to adapt the national economies to international shifts of economic power. In the process the oil-importing developing countries suffered the worst damage of all.

The chaos in international financial relations has contributed to the second deep structural crisis in the international economy in this century, involving:

- Massive unemployment, not just in the developing countries, but in many industrial states too.
- A dangerous increase in isolationism, much to the detriment of the newly industrializing developing countries.
- A fall in the price of commodities which is only partly absorbed.
- Disastrous debts, increased yet further by very high interest rates.

It is hardly surprising that critics observing the situation in the mid-Eighties think it even graver than the great crisis between the two World Wars. Once again we face questions that were to the fore at Bretton Woods. We in the West are not the only ones to feel the lack of a Harry Dexter White and a new Maynard Keynes, the other driving force behind the agreements at the Mount Washington Hotel. They were men with a gift for action as well as analysis, and it was they who worked out the details of the agreements and persuaded their governments to adopt them. They even took pains to ensure that the media could understand their message, and made detailed preparations for the negotiations, devising many clever manoeuvres. Incidentally, only seventeen days were spent on drawing up the terms for the creation of the IMF at Bretton Woods, while for the World Bank it took a whole five!

Today, it is said, things are very much more difficult, and in particular, the political will is lacking. And that is true. But it seems to me that the fundamental question is the same: do we work together or against each other? Despite all obstacles, shall we have cooperation, this time between East and West, North and South (and South and South), or shall we fight each country for itself, all against all, the outcome being uncertain?

The world *needs* a new Bretton Woods, if in a different place. On occasion I have suggested Berlin, politically on the border between East and West, as a suitable scene for such a meeting. For if reform of the international monetary and financial situation were pending, a serious attempt should be made to involve the Soviet Union on the one hand, and to enable the developing countries to participate on genuinely fair terms on the other. At the heart of major reform should be an effort to regulate relations between peoples and states in the name of equality.

The prerequisite would be to abandon that superstitious attitude which expects more of the market than it can deliver. For instance: a few years ago, the big banks protested against any criticism that they were cheerfully allowing developing countries more and more credit without troubling themselves much about their debtors' ability to pay. They presumably believed they were doing right and expected the world's thanks for dealing with a situation that baffled many governments. At first they made some money out of the requisite rescheduling of debts. Moreover, they thought any attempt to subject their operations to international control would only restrict their potential. An American expert remarked pithily, 'Exactly the way bankers argued in my grandfather's time, back in the United States, when national bank regulation was first introduced.'

In fact, too little rather than too much is being invested almost all over the world. But without some kind of regulating authority, the credit boom will get out of control, and the debt crisis can no longer be handled by any government acting alone. In a painful economic crisis, the United States saw the necessity of a controlling hand, and introduced bank regulation. Guidelines are necessary, and so are regulatory supporting actions if the possible collapse of a part is not to destroy the whole. The world economy finds itself in just that danger today. Those institutional safeguards we have at present are not enough to avert the danger.

Now a central authority to administer the world economy is as unlikely to come into being as a world government ruling all the world's different countries. But it is high time for very much closer cooperation and coordination in economic policy, particularly in the areas of currency and credit. The fact is that we are paying for our failure to act when we should have acted, at the time of the first oil shock. That is now over ten years ago. And there is still a good deal of resistance, and people still think along the old lines, advocating the remedies of the day before yesterday. We can see how hard it is to overcome such attitudes even in the narrower sphere of action of the European Community.

The reasons why the world economy finds itself in serious difficulties are of course of very many and very diverse kinds. Obviously none of the various economic theories or schools of thought has the magic formula which would help us to make steady and unproblematic economic progress. And it has become increasingly clear that no model can be put into effect anywhere in what might be called its pure form. So the first essential is for as many as possible of those who have to make the decisions not to let themselves be blinkered by dogma.

The much-vaunted international free trade is not so free at all. Neither world hunger, nor the destruction of the environment, nor the population explosion will stop of their own accord, nor will the arms race be checked by appealing to the free play of market forces. No: what is needed is purposeful concerted action to reach those goals. The same may be said of supplies of energy and commodities, or the control of internationally conditioned inflation and unemployment.

We should look soberly at the call for a new international economic order. I read an article in a French newspaper suggesting that it was time for us to realize that a new order was no longer merely something for the future. The multinational corporations, said the writer, have existed within a new system for quite some while; only politics lag behind the times and fail to provide the essential guidelines appropriate to the new situation. The multinationals succeeded through global planning and cooperation, and they also profited by the competition between governments, basing their activities wherever they found conditions most favourable. Moreover, said the writer, they have also been among the greatest beneficiaries of the monetary confusion of recent years. . . .

The present difficulties call for decisions taking more than the changes of the last few years into account. Governments should not pursue aims that are too contradictory, or adopt measures whose effects will be neutralized in the final analysis. The first essential is not just to talk about international economic inter-dependencies, but to take real account of them; the second is to act accordingly.

Until we have fundamental reform of the international monetary and financial system we must make sure that the Bretton Woods institutions have adequate resources at their disposal to carry out their tasks equitably. Secondly, the developing countries must be given the chance to contribute to their own welfare *and* to the prosperity of the world economy. And thirdly, the industrial countries must try to reach a national consensus, one that will outlast changes of administration, on the outlines of their economic activity, and to achieve coordination of their respective economic policies. Only then can they adjust with any prospect of success to international structural changes and adapt themselves to the modifications necessary. However, we cannot do without a new Bretton Woods.

5. My Experiences on the 'North–South Commission'

In the New Year of 1977, Robert McNamara, then President of the World Bank, sent a messenger to the South of France, where I was on holiday, to ask if he could rely on me to chair an independent commission which he thought was needed. I indicated that my present duties were fairly onerous, but I did not want to respond to this confidence in me with a blunt refusal. A month later McNamara, whom I had known since he was Kennedy's Defence Minister, and whom I had met frequently, both while and after he was at the World Bank, made a speech in

Boston in which he mentioned his idea and my name. I did not make up my mind for some months, but then, at a press conference in New York in late September 1977, I announced my willingness to form, and act as chairman of, an 'Independent Commission on International Development Issues'.

A great many talks preceded this announcement. I was anxious to make it clear that the Commission did not want to complicate government negotiations in any way – a conference on issues of economic cooperation was meeting in Paris until the summer of 1977 – or interfere with the work of international committees. Rather, the group I was to appoint should see its task as making recommendations which would complement activities already in progress, and might help to improve the climate for North–South discussion. I also consulted Kurt Waldheim, then Secretary-General of the United Nations, who said he would be happy to receive the first copy of our report.

I let three considerations guide me in choosing the members of the Commission. First, Third World members should not be numerically in the minority, so that they could not be outvoted. (In fact, there was no voting.) Second, no impression of narrow party political constraint should be allowed to arise: hence we had Edward Heath alongside Olof Palme; along with Eduardo Frei, the Christian Democrat from Chile, a left-wing Algerian Socialist; the militant Commonwealth Secretary-General from Guyana as well as a banker who had been in a Republican administration in the USA; an experienced Indian governor and a Canadian trades union leader. From my exploratory talks, I did not think the time was yet ripe to try recruiting members from the Communist states. Thirdly, I was anxious for the members to be personally responsible for their share in the work, not following directives. We were assured of financial independence also of the World Bank. The government of the Netherlands was guaranteeing our expenses, and bearing half of them; the other half came from contributions made by a number of other countries and institutions.

One of the pleasant surprises of the Commission was that it did succeed in defusing current and future issues in the area of North–South relations of any ideological connotations, and in keeping them free of considerations of national prestige. I found it a fascinating and instructive experience to help in drawing up the report which was published at the beginning of 1980 under the title, *North–South: A Programme for Survival*. This report was translated into more than 20 languages, including Arabic, Chinese, Swahili and Indonesian. A second report, *Common Crisis*, appeared early in 1983.

One cannot say that the two reports failed to have any effect or exert any influence. Initially, they drew a number of comments, some more thoughtful than others, from governments, parliaments and organizations:

- 'We welcome the report of the Brandt Commission, and we shall look carefully at its recommendations,' it was said at the economic summit meeting of the leading Western industrial states in Venice, in June 1980. However, matters rested there.
- Parliaments of various countries and the parliament of the European Community debated the report. Working parties were set up, and several governments redefined their guidelines for development policy in the light of our recommendations, among them the governments of the Federal Republic of Germany, Great Britain and Switzerland. However, no notice was taken of our proposals for fundamental reform.
- International organizations accepted a number of our recommendations. The IMF and the World Bank adopted several of our suggestions – too few, and not quickly enough, but still it was something.
- As for any influence on interested groups and sectors of public opinion, it is hard to gauge. However, over and above serious comment, there were public gatherings with hundreds and even thousands of participants, for instance in Berlin, The Hague, and London. Ten thousand people came to Westminster to take part in a 'lobby on Brandt' and ask members of Parliament to support the report's demands.
- The media in the USA did not take much notice of us, not just because a great deal of attention was then being paid to the renewal of the Cold War. We had underestimated the need for well-organized publicity. However, the main reason might be sought in the change of administration, which also had a

detrimental influence on the effects of the *Global 2000* report in the United States.

Altogether, the immediate effects were restricted in extent. When a few years had passed, and the situation had deteriorated further, some of those ideas which had been dismissed as 'too pessimistic and too radical' were now taken up. Better late than never.

For the rest, I found it was very true that such work cannot be done without a capable secretariat – capable not just technically but in its specialist expertise. Of course it is also true that even the most capable of secretariats needs guidelines. It can perform its function only by reducing the friction between differing schools of thought and different temperaments to a minimum.

It is possible to mitigate but not eliminate the difficulties arising from the fact that a report of this kind must be produced by a number of different authors and editors from among the Commission members. I told some of my colleagues a remark I had just read in the work of an Eastern European dissident: to write a book is far easier for one man than for a collective. Given an authors' collective 40-strong, the writing can become a nightmare. Our own problems were not quite so bad as that.

I countered unreasonable expectations by saying that at worst, we would merely be adding one more book to the literature on development problems, and humanity had known worse things than another publication on a subject of increasing importance. In fact, at least 40 governments referred to our report at the Special General Assembly of the United Nations in 1980. But it was our bad luck to be putting forward our proposals at a time when there was a marked deterioration in the world political situation as a result of the Soviet invasion of Afghanistan and the confused state of affairs in Iran; relations between Washington and Moscow went on deteriorating. When I gave President Carter our report at the beginning of 1980, however, he did express a lively interest in taking some of the heat out of relations with the other superpower. His successor, elected at the end of that year, at the time conveyed no similar impression.

Our report influenced the international debate not so much by way of many separate proposals, as by emphasizing new features in discussions – others as well as ourselves were doing so at this time. We said that conditions for common *survival* were now the main concern, not development *aid* alone, important as that still was; not acts of benevolence, however laudable, but changes made to enable the developing countries to stand on their own feet. The process called for many erroneous ideas to be abandoned.

The Commission could not adopt, sight unseen, the all-inclusive, maximalist demands which many associate with the proposition of a new international economic order. We were unanimous in our view that the time bomb ticking away to the great danger of all could be defused only by making the successful breakthrough to fairly negotiated solutions. An 'all or nothing' approach was and is unrealistic. My colleagues and I settled for a combination of fundamental reforms and smaller steps to put right evils and aberrations. In all likelihood, the requisite changes could not be made in the twinkling of an eye. My reformist credo thus ran: we should keep the broad horizon in view, but not set immediate aims so high as to prohibit all chance of achieving them.

The first Brandt Report included an Emergency Programme for 1980–1985, feeling the world could not be offered long-term measures alone. We listed the equally important elements of the emergency programme as:

- financial aid;
- an international energy strategy;
- a global food programme;
- a start towards some major structural reforms in the international economic system.

An emergency programme of this nature was not meant to be a substitute for longer-term reforms, nor to be inconsistent with them. We said that immediate measures had to be taken if the world economy was not to suffer severely over the next few years. The idea of such a programme was widely discussed, and modified and supplemented, but not put into effect in any appropriate form. It did look as if there might be a chance when a North–

South summit such as we had proposed was envisaged for the autumn of 1981. Unfortunately, the idea did not get far.

6. *The Cancun Summit*

I had strongly advocated occasional summit meetings where serious talks could be held and possible compromises discovered by a limited number of people. Like others, I also realized that no state could make decisions for another at meetings of this nature, and the fundamental equality of all states must remain assured for actual decisions to be taken within the framework of the United Nations. None the less, I felt even more sceptical than many of my colleagues about mammoth conferences.

We therefore agreed that a restricted summit meeting between heads of government from North and South – 'if possible with the participation of the East and China' – might perhaps advance the process of international decision-making. We thought the number of participants should be kept small enough to make progress possible, and large enough to be representative and for what it said to carry weight. 'Such a summit cannot negotiate because it is not universal, nor will it be an appropriate forum to discuss details. But it can reach an understanding on what is necessary, and what is feasible, and how to harmonize the two.'

After laborious preliminary discussions, which I remember only too well, a first such meeting between the leading representatives of 22 states took place in Cancun on the Atlantic coast of Mexico in October 1981. The Austrian Chancellor had agreed to chair it jointly with the President of Mexico. Against all expectations and against advice, the new President of the USA, elected at the end of 1980, also decided to take part. After serious discussion of the invitation – as I was able to ascertain in Moscow in the summer of 1981 – the Russians did not attend. The Chinese were represented by their President, although he said very little. The participating states from the industrial countries were Austria, Canada, France, the Federal Republic of Germany, Japan, Sweden, the United Kingdom, the USA; those from the developing countries were Algeria, Bangladesh, Brazil, China, Guyana,

India, the Ivory Coast, Mexico, Nigeria, the Philippines, Saudi Arabia, Tanzania, Venezuela and Yugoslavia; the UN Secretary-General also attended.

Cancun was adversely affected by the fact that both Bruno Kreisky and Helmut Schmidt were prevented from coming by illness, and had to send representatives. The Canadian premier Pierre Trudeau, who was committed to North–South issues, took the place of the Austrian Chancellor as co-chairman; he was in no way responsible for the unsatisfactory outcome of the meeting.

Commonwealth Secretary-General Ramphal and I had submitted a proposal to the participants which was based on the four points of our emergency programme mentioned above. It laid most emphasis on the need for a global food and agriculture programme, and it did look as if in this area at least, Cancun would make some progress. (At this time, signatures were being collected in the USA for a resolution based on a thesis both brief and to the point: 'If we do not share the world's resources, there will be no justice; without justice there will be no peace; and without peace there will be no freedom anywhere in the world.')

We seemed to have moved closer together in Cancun – for instance, over the framework for the 'global' negotiations upon which the United Nations had decided in the autumn of 1979, though nothing much ever came of them. Important issues in the areas of commodities, energy, trade, development, currency and finance should be discussed, within their contexts. There was fundamental agreement on this point at the summit, even from the President of the USA, but subsequently, again, nothing happened. None the less, I and some others were inclined to consider Cancun a modest, partial success. At least one could learn from it.

I had comprehensive talks with three Presidents of the UN General Assembly – my countryman Rüdiger von Wechmar, the Iraqi ambassador Kittani, ambassador Muños Ledo of Mexico – and with the Secretary-General of the United Nations, on the difficulty of initiating global negotiations. In previous years, everything had seemed to founder on the fact that some spokesmen for the developing countries gave an impression of wanting to decide the future of institutions such as the IMF, and the policy to be followed by the industrial countries, by the force of their majority vote alone. Later, however, some very moderate and constructive proposals put forward by the non-aligned countries and the Group of 77 foundered on the delaying tactics of the US government and its hard-core allies.

In practical terms, the proposal was to depart from the idea of a vast 'global' round of negotiations and to tackle particularly urgent problems in an initial phase, concentrating on those areas where it was likely that consensus could be reached. In a second phase, attention could be turned to the really difficult problems, particularly those dealing with structural and institutional changes. From the angle of negotiating techniques, this combination of gradual progress and extensive discussion should be supplemented by an understanding on regional representation between the various governments, so that effective working parties could be set up. The influence of the moderate developing countries, led by India, melted away when their concessions – formally as well as in fact – were not honoured.

After the Cancun summit, President Reagan thanked me for the contribution of the North–South Commission. He emphasized the importance of development aid for many countries, insisting that private investment should play a greater part. The IMF and the World Bank, he said, were trying to put the resources available to even more efficient use. . . . None of this sounded hostile, but it did leave a basic question unanswered. In the poorest countries, the alternatives of private investment and public aid simply do not exist. As with the conflict of dogmas between free market and centrally planned economies, financial issues run the risk of arguing about non-existent alternatives. More private or more public investment? More multilateral or more bilateral lending? In fact both are needed. (The World Bank, which in any case is the largest borrower on private markets, is considered by experts more efficient than many of the internationally active commercial banks, as we are told in a US Congress study. That does not affect the necessity for reforms, for nothing is so good that it cannot be improved.)

The idea of resorting to summit meetings as an instrument – not just summit meetings of the great powers – has not perished. I have already mentioned the matters on Indira Gandhi's mind in the months before her assassination. It is not impossible that a selected group of heads of government may meet again to discuss certain precisely defined North–South issues (and their connection with East–West issues). The number of participants in such discussions should be kept to a genuine minimum. A certain amount of preparation is called for, but above all crucial questions must be discussed, and opinions on practical proposals exchanged. For the rest, it is an error refuted by experience for certain types of high-ranking civil servants to suppose that the future of the world depends on their rituals and compromise formulas, the leaders really being there only to read out prepared speeches, give their blessing to press releases on matters already negotiated, and observe the obligatory forms of protocol.

Security policy and North–South relations are matters too serious to be left to such officials alone, be they ever so competent. Or to put it less kindly: the leaders must not be let off the hook of doing their duty.

7. *Proposals*

No one can say that the recommendations of my Commission, particularly in the areas of development finance and monetary issues, are notable for radicalism. However, they have aroused a certain sense of discomfort. That was inevitable, in their very nature.

Reform of the international monetary system should, in our judgment, improve international liquidity and exchange rate stability, and also the reserve system and balance of payments adjustment, and should, moreover, ensure the participation of the *whole* international community of states in future cooperation: 'Mechanisms should be agreed for creating and distributing an international currency to be used for clearing and settling outstanding balances between central banks. Such a currency would replace the use of national currencies as international reserves.'

This international currency is envisaged as an improved Special Drawing Right.* We suggested creating new SDRs to the extent

---

* Special Drawing Rights, or SDRs, are the IMF's currency equivalent, and were introduced in 1969 as the first step towards an international reserve currency. Since 1981 the value of a Special Drawing Right has been calculated daily on the basis of a 'basket' of the five main currencies of the member states.

required by the need for increased (and as far as possible non-inflationary) world liquidity. The developing countries, we said, should have preferential treatment in the distribution of new liquidity, the process of adjustment should be accelerated, and should be seen in the larger context of furthering economic and social development in the long term.

The IMF should avoid 'inappropriate or excessive regulation of the economies' of the developing countries, and 'should not impose highly deflationary measures as standard adjustment policy'. Apart from various technical details, we wanted to further 'the demonetization of gold'; profits from the sale of gold should be used for the benefit of developing countries. We called on both the IMF and the World Bank to increase participation by the developing countries in their staffing, management and decision-making.

In our supplementary report, published early in 1983, we concentrated on these proposals. We repeated our call for the capital of the World Bank to be enlarged (to a modest extent, this was done), and for the 'gearing ratio' – the ratio of borrowing to capital – to be raised from 1:1 to 2:1.

In both reports, we referred to the 0.7 per cent target. In accordance with a decision of the UN General Assembly in October 1970, previously formulated at the first UNCTAD conference in Geneva in 1964, at least 0.7 per cent of the gross national product of the industrial countries should be made available for Official Development Assistance (ODA). We made other detailed recommendations. Here are a few comments on what actually happened:

- Instead of increasing Official Development Assistance to 0.7 per cent or even perhaps 1 per cent of GNP, several of the rich countries have moved yet further away from the 0.7 per cent target. At the beginning of the Eighties, the real value of development aid had sunk in both absolute and relative terms.
- At the 1983 UNCTAD conference in Belgrade, the USA, the Eastern bloc and New Zealand rejected the 0.7 per cent target in principle; the delegation of the Federal Republic of Germany was not empowered to agree to a fixed commitment.
- The Federal Republic of Germany did, however, approach the

0.5 per cent mark (0.49 per cent in 1985), while the North as a whole did not get above 0.36 per cent.

- In 1983 the net disbursements of the Western industrial countries amounted to 27.3 billion dollars (down by half a billion compared to the previous year), a good 12 billion dollars being accounted for by the World Bank group.
- Japan, whose performance in this respect had long been below average, has made efforts to increase its contribution over the last few years.
- The Netherlands and the Scandinavian countries, which voluntarily set themselves the 1 per cent target, have recently had difficulty in fitting it into their budgets.
- It must be borne in mind that only about 10 per cent gross investment of the developing countries are financed through Official Development Assistance. Thus they are financing the bulk of their investment with domestic savings.

The effectiveness of development aid has been considerably reduced or inhibited by:

- an increase in debts and in interest rates (the dollar exchange rate!),
- high oil prices,
- the market strategies of transnational corporations,
- armaments exports, including those forced upon countries.

At a conference in Paris in the autumn of 1981 a praiseworthy – and at first not entirely fruitless – attempt was made to stabilize assistance for the *poorest* countries, that is, those too poor to be able to incur any debts at all on the international capital market. It was agreed to double the aid for the 36 poorest countries until 1984; these countries included Ethiopia, Somalia, the Sudan, Tanzania, Afghanistan, Bangladesh, both the Yemens, Laos, Nepal and Haiti. At least 0.15 per cent of the GNP of the donor countries was intended to go to these poorest of the poor. In point of fact, the situation in these countries has deteriorated yet further.

The only countries to adhere to the agreed 0.15 per cent were Denmark, the Netherlands, Norway and Sweden. The Federal

Republic of Germany managed 0.12 per cent. The average was only 0.08 per cent. The failure in the replenishment of funds for the International Development Association (IDA, affiliated to the World Bank) placed a further burden on the poorest countries. And for another thing, checks must constantly be made to see whether the resources available are being effective.

When my colleagues and I spoke of the provision of additional funds, we were thinking of:

- first, an international system of progressive taxation, with the participation of the Eastern European states and the developing countries – excepting, however, the poorest;
- secondly, automatic generation of revenue (on a principle similar to that of indirect national taxation) by means of modest international charges which might be levied on, say, the manufacture or export of armaments, as well as on mankind's common property, in particular the resources of the sea-bed. International tourism and air traffic, as well as the utilization of space, were also mentioned as possible points of reference. (I will add here, as I have said before, that I do *not* think a country's share of world trade a suitable criterion.)

The creation of a new institution to provide finance, a 'World Development Fund', was also discussed. It would be supported by universal membership and act as a channel for such funds as were automatically raised worldwide. Despite doubts expressed not only by right-wing conservative and conservative left-wing governments, but in the upper echelons of the existing institutions, this idea should be given further consideration. The proposal worked out by our secretariat did not aim to replace existing institutions but to complement them, thus establishing credit policy on a broader basis. It has clearly been indicated that the credit flow into the developing countries from commercial banks and other private sources of finance should be increased at the same time.

We firmly believed that additional, multinational finance was needed for exploring and exploiting sources of energy and mineral resources in those developing countries not in a position to do it by themselves. The 'Energy Agency' we suggested for this purpose was in practical terms the only new organization whose immediate creation, with the support of the World Bank, we proposed. At first its chances looked quite good. Then the man at the head of one of the big oil companies turned to the American President (whose name did not happen to be Reagan at the time) and suggested to him that governments should keep out of a domain considered the property of the big corporations, on an international as well as a national level (even when they were inactive where, as in some of the smaller developing countries, there was little prospect of profits).

On the subject of *commodities*, my Commission recommended greater participation by the developing countries in their processing, marketing and distribution. We thought that measures to stabilize commodity prices should be undertaken as a matter of urgency. Work on an 'integrated' programme, financed by a Common Fund, had been in progress since 1973. We wanted such a fund to be enabled to encourage and finance effective International Commodity Agreements. National stockpiling should be encouraged too, so that commodities could be advantageously processed and marketed. Negotiations on individual commodity agreements should be brought, we said, to a rapid and successful conclusion. This was exactly what did not happen.

The work of the Fund should have begun on 1 January 1984. The Federal Republic of Germany agreed to it in the spring of 1985. But the necessary number of ratifications was not forthcoming, and the Eastern states were hesitant. It was feared, and not just in America, that commodity regulation – from coffee to cotton, from tin to copper – would pave the way for an international centrally planned economy. Should one forgo the doubtful chance of profiting from price fluctuations?

Anyone with an interest in calculability and guaranteed commodity supplies ought not at heart to be against remunerative and relatively stable commodity prices – if only because of the investment required to open up mineral resources. (When an outcry went up at the first steep rise in oil prices, at the end of 1973, most of the vociferous critics would not admit that the oil-producing countries had been defrauded over a number of years by prices which were objectively speaking too low; also, and inevitably, there was the widely and mistakenly held view that an inexhaustible supply existed.) One may, indeed one must, ask what happens to the people of a country whose government has to use a very large part of its export earnings for servicing its debts. What good is it to them if they have to pay for an imported tractor (or dollar) with an ever-increasing quantity of coffee or sugar? What is the effect on the people of Zambia if, with all her copper, she can only just manage to service her debts?

At the end of the Seventies there was a considerable drop in commodity prices. In Zambia we saw on the spot that the low prices for copper had not obtained since the Thirties. Compared with a few years earlier, the developing countries had to export twelve times as much coffee and twenty times as much sugar, and very many times as much sisal, to buy one and the same barrel of oil. At the beginning of 1984, even the Kissinger Commission, in its report on Central America, observed that the region was having to export twice as much as five years before in order to buy the same goods on the world market.

On the subject of *world trade*, we wanted to give the developing countries more opportunities, so that they could contribute to their own welfare *and* the welfare of the world economy. Among other things, our suggestions included:

- the concluding of commodity agreements, as already mentioned, which would contribute to the stabilization of prices and markets;
- improved access to the markets of the industrial countries, since only thus could the developing countries be able to buy goods for themselves or pay their debts;
- greater support for those developing countries making efforts to increase their production of food and energy.

We wanted effective national laws and international codes of conduct to prevent *transnational corporations* from indulging in restrictive business practices, and at the same time to have a positive influence on the transfer of technology. We thought these *multinationals*, in themselves, neither good nor bad, but we did query their conduct, their role and their accountability. Do they keep within the law? Do they invest a good part of their profits in the host countries? Do they have links only with an élite, or do they keep the interests of large sections of society in view? I shall be returning to this subject. The question is not whether a corporation does or does not have a transnational structure, but what is done with it.

For the rest, we firmly stated that permanent sovereignty over their natural resources is the right of all countries. However, it is necessary that nationalization be accompanied by appropriate and effective compensation, under internationally compatible principles. These principles, we said, should be embodied in national laws and increasing use should also be made of international mechanisms for settling disputes.

We also supported the view that greater efforts – international, regional and national – were needed to promote the *development of technology* in Third World countries. The transfer of technology should be supported 'at reasonable prices'. In saying this, we agreed that there is a cost factor, but said nothing about the function and cost of technologies that are 'appropriate' or 'conform to the situation', which are all the more important the less room there is for suspecting that conformity of such a kind is a way of perpetuating structural backwardness and traditional dependence. The fact that cost-effectiveness is also a problem when money is spent on foreign experts is so self-evident that it is sometimes overlooked.

8. *Diktat or dialogue*

In the spring of 1984 I was to speak on the occasion of a rather curious anniversary. It was a hundred years since Imperial Germany made a brief foray into colonial history. The birthday of the German colonies is taken to be 24 April 1884. On that day, Bismarck telegraphed the German consul in Cape Town saying that the acquisitions of the businessman Lüderitz to the north of the Orange River should henceforth enjoy German protection. In the same year, Herr Nachtigal claimed Togo and Cameroon for the Reich, and a year later Carl Peters's acquisitions came under Imperial protection as German East Africa.

The end of 1884 saw the opening in Berlin of what is known as the Congo Conference, at which the interested powers agreed on the creation of a 'free trade zone' in Central Africa. This led among other things, and without the participation of any African representatives, to the founding of the Belgian Congo, under the sovereignty of the King of the Belgians. The interests of German liquor exporters were also concerned. The document drawn up at the close of the conference spoke of high aims; the intention was 'to create the most favourable of conditions for the development of trade and civilization in certain regions of Africa in a harmonious spirit of mutual understanding, and to obviate misunderstandings and disputes which might arise later from the occupation of further territories on the African coasts'. This document was 'mindful of finding the means to increase the moral and material welfare of the native tribes'.

All the interested powers had accepted the joint German and French invitation to Berlin. Besides the two hosts, the following were assembled in a pleasing spirit of concord: Belgium, Britain, Denmark, Italy, the Netherlands, Portugal, Russia, Sweden, the United States and the Ottoman Empire, now Turkey. What happened on that occasion in Berlin, a hundred years ago, was a case of unconcealed *Diktat* in the field later known as North–South relations. There was little criticism of the governments' actions. In the Reich, few people apart from Social Democrats thought colonial policy wrong or reprehensible. Things have changed since then, but it is not by any means certain that we can speak of *dialogue* rather than *Diktat* with a clear conscience today.

Dialogue is certainly not as yet the simple and clear alternative in North–South relations. In recent years some people have spoken – not unreasonably – of a dialogue between the deaf, or the delivery of parallel monologues. In addition, there is no strong lobby for development policy. However, even leaving aside moral objections, supposing they *can* be left aside, circumstances are not much longer in any way appropriate for *Diktat*.

Some feel concern at talk of partnership in development, reasonably enough envisaging unequal partners, and fearing that the phrase conceals the attempt to impose a *Diktat* by gentler but no less compelling means. And no doubt some of those involved

will see it in that way too. Such attitudes must be firmly countered, for instance by greater participation of the Third World in
the control of the international institutions. However, that cannot be done just by putting someone with the 'right' passport in a
given place. (It is said that every one of the 'Chicago Boys' in
Santiago is a Chilean.)

Nothing much will come, either, of drawing up as comprehensive as possible a catalogue of subjects for negotiation, making it
clear that no issue is to be decided in isolation. The decisive
factors are the attitude of those involved and the guidelines to
which the negotiators must keep. Anyone who sees North–South
relations only in terms of demands made by one side or the other
basically misunderstands the question. And mutual interests
cannot be defined or perceived in that way either. A *Diktat* is no
kind of model for the future. As for dialogue – so far, only a few
starts have been made, but that way hope lies.

Meanwhile we are facing a situation very considerably affected
by new forces – forces which did not previously exist, and which
draw their significance from new technical developments. What is
often seen as government weakness is in many cases nothing but
inability to control or deal with such new forces: multinational
corporations, the international network of experts in the technology of the future, trades unions and other social groupings,
churches, solidarity movements.

The importance and influence of such actors on the scene is
increasing, and they are largely outside political control, particularly when their activities cross frontiers, while governments are
hampered by the illusion of sovereignty. The part played by these
new actors rests to a great extent on the frontier-crossing mobility
of factors of production: goods, capital, technology and labour,
despite all trends in the opposite direction, have an international
market which is not decisively influenced by governments. That
does not mean governments are not called upon at times of crisis,
particularly when it is a question of unloading losses on the
general public and transferring them to the taxpayer.

In the introduction to the first Brandt Report, I wrote that the
shaping of our common future was too important to be left to
governments and experts alone: 'Therefore, our appeal goes to
youth, to women's and labour movements; to political, intellec-

tual and religious leaders; to scientists and educators; to technicians and managers; to members of the rural and business communities. May they all try to understand and to conduct their affairs in the light of this new challenge.'

To put it even more clearly: pressure must be brought to bear on governments. If the moral reserves of many individuals are mobilized in favour of a development policy worthy of the name, that will be a help, and if besides complaints of the cumbersome nature of the decision-making process we also hear denunciation of the pettiness and frigidity not infrequently observed to accompany it, that will help too. (Development aid is not, of course, exactly at the top of the list of those issues that decide elections. Holland and the Scandinavian countries are good examples of the way a well-planned programme of public information can elicit a positive response. In the Federal Republic of Germany, we lag some way behind. In addition, a comparatively small circle of interested persons dispute the finer points among themselves, instead of getting together in the first place to canvass for more interest, commitment and resources.)

The way out of our present dilemma obviously does not lie in new international super-bureaucracies. Enough confusion reigns in those which already exist. But setting up a new institution to deal with an important and clearly defined area is a possibility. A thorough reform of existing institutions is more important, however. That applies not only to the United Nations and its specialized organizations. Internationally and nationally alike, bureaucracy proliferates. However, it is the governments of member states which bear responsibility for such a development in international institutions. With this in view, they should be called to a sense of their obligations by their national parliaments.

When the United Nations was created towards the end of the Second World War, it had roughly one third of its present number of member states. Since then, not only have many new nation-states come into being, there has also been a considerable fragmentation of the political map of the world. A large number of new states reflect the territorial boundaries of their colonial past; this is particularly clear in Africa. Which means that they often have to live with frontiers that are felt to be artificial. State sovereignty, which in many cases can be described as national sovereignty only with reservations, is supposed to be of primary importance. However, to respect frontiers once drawn is at the same time a prerequisite of regional cooperation.

Yet we live at a time when technical development, in what is in some ways a revolutionary manner, reduces the objective importance of state frontiers. A large part of international transactions takes place outside those controls which the authorities in individual states would like to or are able to exercise. That becomes especially clear when one realizes that the United Nations now has a long list of member states with less than one million inhabitants, some even with less than 100,000. On the one hand we have the United States and the Soviet Union, China and India; on the other we have Fiji and Papua New Guinea, the Maldives, St Kitts and Nevis. One can see at a glance how limited the areas must be in which equal voting rights are anything but a fiction.

Gunnar Myrdal, some years ago, pointed out the paradox of a situation wherein on the one hand states try to regulate their economic life, but on the other must take note of the fact that an increasing amount of production and trade is now removed from their control, and even their knowledge. There is no doubt that a growing economic and financial interdependence has developed internationally. Governments have not succeeded in bringing transnational companies under control through appropriate forms of cooperation, let alone in helping to coordinate the activities of trades unions. Even the international exchange of data for fiscal purposes has not proved particularly effective.

It is beginning to be said that the political autonomy of a state – independence is often a misleading notion anyway – should not be confused with its economic autonomy. Dependence, including dependence of an indirect nature, is made particularly obvious by the debt crisis. International organizations are ineffective because considerable elements of sovereignty of the great powers and influential states are hardly being delegated to the international plane.

However I do not look at global interdependency and jump to the conclusion that the creation of some kind of world government might be on the agenda. That will be kept waiting. And the matter is more complicated than it appears to many well-meaning people. Nor, if we are aiming at sensible objectives, can it be just a case of common action in the face of global challenges. It is equally important to define decentralized *regional* responsibilities, which probably is in the interests of the mini-states. It will be hard enough to overcome narrow-minded opposition to such ideas.

On the way towards a higher degree of common responsibility, questions concerning the point of big international conferences force themselves upon us:

- What can come of a meeting of several thousand people from a large number of countries, unless some provision is made to divide them up into working groups?
- Could not ministers stay at home and have copies of their speeches distributed, if their only reason for attending is to read those speeches, and then set off straight back home, perhaps after a few social events – leaving behind them civil servants without any authority to make decisions?
- Should not the UN General Assembly itself make efforts to set limits to the time allowed for the delivery of speeches? Is it not an illusion when the majority decides matters which the great powers, or groups of states, see as touching on their vital interests?

In many respects, technology is showing a tendency to run ahead of politics. It is as well to be aware of this, and compensate for it where possible.

9. *Must Europe Wait on the Will of the Superpowers?*

It would not be right to accuse others of failing to take their responsibilities seriously enough, and then fall considerably short of what we expect of others. We in Europe cannot hold our heads up if we shelter behind Russian obstinacy or American stubbornness, instead of asking ourselves about our own responsibility. If the superpowers will not accept advice from anyone, that does not mean others must accept all they are told. Nor need they go along with all that they are expected to do. They have to speak out where their convictions and understanding demand it. In the final resort, we too must pay for the mistakes of the great powers.

On fundamental issues I do not share the opinion of those who wield power in the Eastern bloc. We also have serious differences of opinion with regard to the treatment of North–South problems. I live in the West and belong to the West, and I know what strength we draw from the opportunities of a pluralistic system. It no longer bothers me to find reformist policies regarded as suspect. But one does notice the way people are dismissed as fools or worse for years on end, if they do not go along with every dangerous piece of nonsense, praising it as a manifestation of the utmost wisdom, as long as it comes from Washington.

I agree with Helmut Schmidt when he called upon the other industrial states to help the poorest countries even if the United States refuses to continue doing its part. That was with reference to the dispute in 1984 centering upon the International Development Association, affiliated to the World Bank, a dispute which led to a reduction in the opportunities for helping the poorest developing countries.

I say here, again: those who have power, particularly nuclear power, do not necessarily have morality or wisdom on their side. The great dangers to mankind proceed from the great powers, not the little ones.

In recent years, unfortunately, no more initiatives in the field of North–South politics have come from the USA, which in the Fifties was canvassing the Europeans for cooperation in development policy. There has been a lack of positive decisions, and the connection between arms and development has not been accepted; instead, we have seen a series of negative decisions and delaying tactics.

There is little point in vociferously drawing exaggerated conclusions from these regrettable facts, or in uttering condemnations. And in particular, it should never be forgotten that the USA disburses considerable funds for foreign aid earmarked for specific purposes. First and foremost, we should strive for more understanding in the USA itself of what many of their friends in Europe and the Third World expect of them. Consequently, the Americans should be invited to participate in renewed collaboration; they should not have the door slammed in their faces, nor be made the subject of hurtful criticism. That, however, cannot mean standing by, come what may; we should do as we think right in a given situation, even if we cannot do it (or cannot yet do it) in the larger context that was envisaged.

If I am critical in my attitude to United States policy, it is as 'one of the family'. Also as one who is sorry that official sources in Bonn do not say what ought to be said to official sources in Washington. Also as a European.

This concerns the European Community, and at the same time it concerns the stance taken by Europeans beyond the Community. For decades, particularly since the Second World War, there has been talk of de-Europeanizing the world. I think it may be said that that is followed, if slowly and as a contradictory process, by a Europeanization of Europe, including that part of it dominated by the Soviet Union. Over the last few years there has been more than one indication that European governments in East and West – with all their great differences, and with all the loyalties they feel to their respective alliances – have found a *common* interest in their wish not to bear too much of the brunt of extreme tension between the superpowers.

In any event, Europeans – or quite a number of them – will be less anxious than before to reject the idea of exercising a moderating influence in crisis areas, and will not want to leave those areas entirely to the superpowers. Our European contribution to ensuring peace must not lag so far behind opportunity as it has for a long while since the end of the Second World War. It is hard to see why it should, since Europe would be more likely and more intensively than any other region to become the actual arena of a nuclear catastrophe.

Europe might have a chance of pointing out new paths and taking them herself. It is to be feared that she will miss that chance, particularly with so many spanners being thrown into the works of the EEC. There is not much time left. Talk of the unification of Europe is nothing new, but little has come of it so far. And yet, over and above economic matters and a considerable share of world trade, the twelve states which today constitute the EEC have made some progress in coordinating their foreign policies. Something might yet come of that, if we do not delay too long.

Europe should have made her mark in development policy by her own efforts – working together, as appropriate, with Japan, or Canada, or Australia, or other countries. She might have been able to launch initiatives of her own, with practical projects. She should have dared to believe herself capable of a mediating role in getting serious negotiations going within the framework of the United Nations. Nor could anyone seriously have prevented Europe – I now mean in the sense of those various dimensions which go beyond EEC limits – from taking a clear lead in the fight against hunger.

Or we can start from more modest premises, and ask: why have the Western European governments not even managed to coordinate their activities in development policy better? Why are the already hard-pressed administrations of the developing countries, particularly the least developed, called upon to put up with such a vast quantity of parallel negotiations, visits and project surveys? Why must 20 ministers with responsibility for development cooperation visit the same countries, claiming the attention of their administrations, usually close on one another's heels? (And followed by civil servants from rival ministries and audit offices, and delegates of various committees, from almost all of those separate countries.) Political as well as technical coordination is needed! The European Parliament is in favour of it. The parliamentary assembly of the Council of Europe has endorsed the idea as well, and described the form it should take.

The EEC has had a good deal of experience, if nothing very exciting in the way of results, with the Lomé Conventions. These agreements concern previously dependent areas of Africa, the Caribbean and the Pacific: the ACP states, at present numbering over 60 members. A renewal of the Convention, to apply to the current five-year period, was signed in Lomé, the capital of Togo, at the end of 1984. The volume of finance provided – with a per capita drop – is in the order of DM 19 billion. In addition there are marginal concessions regulating access to the EEC market. Results have not come up to expectations, and not only the expectations of those who know that the EEC's agrarian market costs it DM 40 billion *annually*.

None the less, the Lomé Conventions, to which special regional agreements are attached, have features which could be useful as models in further North–South dialogue. Such is the case with the principle of aid for self-help, and with the Stabex mechanism, which involves compensatory payments for severe losses in export revenue to help mitigate the dependency from unbalanced export structures. It is also the case with environmental protection, which is at last, through regional projects and long-term programmes, taking on great importance. Despite all the criticism of governments which are behind the times, it should not be forgotten that the EEC has good dispositions for performance in development policies.

Much is still expected – or is again expected – of Europe. I sensed that in Latin America, just as I did in China and India, the Near East, Africa, and the other parts of the Third World. Sometimes one found it surprising that Europe, with all her inadequacies, still seems so attractive. Expectations are often pitched too high, and could hardly be fulfilled even if conditions were more favourable. But still, those expectations can be an incentive to regard goodwill as a positive challenge. Instead of complaining of lack of leadership from the great powers, we should have had the courage to go ahead ourselves – for instance, with a plan for long-term aid to Africa, with some kind of Marshall Plan for Latin America, with a perspective of productive global cooperation.

In an interdependent world, the principles of common justice and the general welfare cannot cease to hold good at our own frontiers. I believe we must do more in the way of cooperation, and indeed make more of an effort in many respects, without expecting miracles to occur overnight. But greater generosity will pay dividends.

VI

THE INTERNATIONAL DEVELOPMENT
ASSOCIATION SCANDAL

In 1984 the World Bank tried to increase the funding of interest-free loans to those developing countries with particularly weak economies, or at least to make sure that it did not decrease. In the committees of the World Bank, the majority of governments agreed upon a middle way. However, the United States administration steadfastly refused to compromise. For the period 1985–87, consequently, there is less money available (when inflation has been taken into account) than for the three preceding years; not much more than half the previous sum, while the population of the countries eligible for this type of credit has practically doubled – for China is now among their number, and does not want to be treated any differently from India.

When this happened, the governments of Europe and Japan did not say they would stand by their word. Instead, they renounced any idea of an initiative of their own, and allowed an important area of development policy to suffer. I have called the argument over the International Development Association (IDA) a scandal, and I see no reason to withdraw that term.

The report of my Commission suggested that governments should make their contributions to IDA on at least a five-year instead of a three-year basis. We also said it was important that no political conditions were attached to the use of these funds. A large replenishment for the 1985–87 period would have contributed greatly to achieving the objective of increased aid for the poorest countries. In 1981, a conference was held in Paris, attended by the representatives of those countries whose economic development is declining and which receive less aid. It was agreed to double official development assistance to the countries by 1985. Both expectations and promises have remained largely unfulfilled.

At the beginning of January 1984, at the joint meeting of the Brandt and Palme Commissions, it was established that negotiations over IDA replenishment to date had lowered the amount actually available to below the sum many donor countries were ready to contribute. In view of the needs of the poorest countries, the amount of the agreed contributions was wholly inadequate: 'We support the proposal already put forward whereby IDA resources should be raised to at least $12 billion. We shall do everything we can to encourage the donor countries to change their attitude to one more worthy of the international community.'

What had happened? IDA funds for 1982–84 had been set at $9 billion. The World Bank, which is not prone to exaggeration, thought an increase to $16 billion was called for; the committees agreed on $12 billion. Thereupon, the USA said that they were not going to participate: they could undertake to contribute their 25 per cent share only of the previously agreed $9 billion, i.e. $750 million of the annual $3 billion. (The disputed $250 million per year would have amounted to less than 0.1 per cent of the US defence budget.)

The cutting down on replenishment means that in real terms there are now considerably less resources available than was the case in recent years, even though the need for them has grown: for another thing, the vast country of China is now a World Bank member and thus eligible to apply.

Together with Ted Heath and Sonny Ramphal, I turned to a number of heads of government. We received a predominantly friendly response – from Washington as well as the rest. We had appealed to President Reagan to change his administration's stance. He did not exclude the possibility of reviewing it in the next American fiscal year. However, there was no mention of any such review in the draft of the administration's next budget.

It cannot have been the money alone; another factor will have been the increasing efforts being made by the United States, in a spirit rather far removed from the principles of the immediate postwar period, to weaken rather than strengthen international organizations, replacing multilateral by bilateral agreements.

This generally means that the stronger party to the agreement is not really practising partnership, but is imposing conditions on the weaker party.

The European states that we asked to keep their word to the World Bank, making their contributions within the $12 billion context even after Washington's withdrawal, could not make up their minds to do so. Personal mediation in Bonn and Paris had no effect.

I do not gather the impression that anything very pointed was ever said to the Americans, as envisaged before the economic summit in London in the early summer of 1984. Chancellor Kohl had written to me in September 1984, saying that he too considered $9 billion 'too little' for IDA's seventh replenishment. But, he said, in view of the American attitude, it had not been feasible to fix a higher sum. In common with Japan, official opinion in Bonn was 'that a supplementary fund without the participation of the USA would have rather negative effects'. Only mutual understanding between all donor countries, he said, had led to the impressive contributions to early replenishments. In the interests of the developing countries, the same system of raising contributions should be retained for the future. The Federal Government had repeatedly made it clear that 'it could not make up deficits arising from the non-participation of a third party'. I was not convinced by these formal considerations, nor by the tactics involved, if tactics they be. Upholding the traditional way of distributing the load might once have made sense, as a means of persuading the US to participate, but today it is clearly to the disadvantage of the poorest countries (and allows hypocrites in Europe to save money).

At the annual meeting of the IMF and the World Bank in Washington, in September 1984, it was proposed to raise an additional $2 billion to relieve poverty in Africa. One may wonder why it was necessary to commission new 'studies' for this purpose first. A few months later, Tom Clausen, President of the World Bank, announced that it was hoped a special programme of at least $1 billion for the poorest African states could be decided on at the beginning of 1985. Meanwhile, the USA had again made it clear that they were not particularly interested in joint programmes; however, they said they would increase their own aid to Africa. In the meantime, the summit conference of OAU, the Organization of African Unity, could refer to the World Bank and their projected $2 billion a year. . . .

When President Clausen was canvassing for aid for Africa at the end of 1984, he put it to the rich countries, in front of the Press in Washington, that they might spend less on armaments and let the Third World countries have more resources instead.

However, it proved impossible to set up even the African programme as envisaged. Abdulatif Al Hamad, the Kuwaiti member of the Brandt Commission, raised a good half billion dollars for the World Bank, and the sum was made up to $1.1 billion by the inclusion of parallel national contributions. Washington's decision to set up its own programme caused Bonn to pull out too, announcing that it was making its own contribution of DM 100 million – provided by the reprogramming of funds already pledged. On the other hand, France, Italy and the Netherlands, among the EEC countries, did make direct contributions to the World Bank's Special Aid Fund.

It is worth setting the shameful result of the efforts made to raise money for the poorest countries against two striking comparisons: first, the German Federal Bank spent $1.5 billion within a week in order to stabilize the exchange rate of the Deutschmark; the net amount of currency reserves fell by that sum in the first week of March 1985. And secondly: every eight or nine hours, the world spends $1 billion – i.e. the entire sum provided for the Special Africa Programme – on armaments and for military purposes. That comes to almost three Africa Programmes a day, and it happens every day of the year. . . .

VII

DEBTS AND HYPOCRISY

1. *Debts upon Debts*

At the turn of the year between 1984 and 1985, the total indebtedness of the Third World was estimated to be in the region of $920 billion; some estimates made it as much as $1,000 billion. At least $360 billion of that amount – between a third and a half of it – fell to the share of Latin America.

Hence, Latin America's burden of debt became the focus of interest; it was its severest economic crisis this century, and has resulted in a distinct drop in the standard of living over the last ten years.

In September 1982, the tip of the iceberg showed in Mexico. An important country producing a considerable amount of oil, Mexico had become insolvent. The acute insolvency was pretty quietly eased, but turned out to be the start of a severe crisis which has not gone away. An eminent participant in the annual meeting of the IMF and the World Bank in Toronto in 1982 has spoken of the alarm he sensed 'when Mexico was seen to be insolvent and we didn't know if the whole situation might explode at any moment'. Those who handled the crisis did remarkable work: 800 foreign banks had to be induced to keep quiet. In addition to considerable interest payments they were compensated with fees of notable size in compensation.

The overnight Mexican collapse had been set off by changes in the oil market. Large finds were made in 1976–80, and on the assumption of high prices exports had been overestimated. In other parts other factors triggered the debt crisis. The international financial world felt not just alarm but almost as if the end of the world had come when, in the summer of 1983, Brazil refused to make its repayment due to the Bank for International Settlements in Basle: so said no less a person than the Swiss banker at the head of the BIS itself. There was another collapse to be averted in the spring of 1984, when Argentina had to be granted a bridging loan, a loan notable for the fact that – besides the USA – states participated, or were obliged to participate, which, like Mexico, were themselves deeply in debt.

These cases were not the only ones of their kind. Bolivia and Ecuador temporarily suspended the servicing of their debts. A call for a political solution came from the new democratic government in Buenos Aires. Other capitals echoed this demand, and in some quarters consideration was given to the idea of a debtors' cartel with the help of which at least a moratorium – that is, a deferment – might be enforced.

The real problems had arisen when short-term funds were used to finance long-term investments; the exceptional case turned out to be the rule. Unexpectedly high interest rates and export difficulties played their part. A greater and greater share of budgets and export revenues had to go to the servicing of debts.

Over the last few years, the world has seen an explosion of public debt. Everywhere – in small states and large ones, in industrial and developing countries, in the North and South, in the East and West – there was a similar rise in public debt, be it through internal financing in the industrialized countries or financing from outside in the developing countries, in some states in the East, and latterly in the USA. In the summer of 1984 the managing director of the IMF revealed that in the seven major Western industrial states, the ratio of national debt to gross national product had risen from 22 per cent in 1974 to 41 per cent in 1983. The debt crisis of the Third World thus coincided with high public indebtedness in the industrial countries. Some of those statesmen dispensing moralizing advice to the developing countries looked like drunkards preaching abstinence.

As compared with the situation ten years ago, the developing countries must now pay more in annual interest – over $100 billion – than the total amount of their debts then. (The African states alone are in debt to the tune of over $150 billion.) The annual debt service comes to three times the value of annual development aid from the West. Another and striking statistical comparison: the balance of payments deficits of the oil-importing developing countries have increased tenfold since the beginning of the Sixties.

Also in 1984 a considerable quantity of new debts was incurred, even if the proportion of short-term debts distinctly dropped. The fact that the Eastern bloc managed to decrease its international burden of debt brought about some changes. Between the spring of 1982 and the spring of 1984, the indebtedness of the Eastern bloc dropped by 14 per cent to $51 billion, and deposits made by those countries with international banks rose to $9 billion. Even Poland managed to decrease her debts during that period, though not in 1985. At the end of 1984 non-aligned Yugoslavia managed to obtain assurances from her creditors, that debt service payments, some $20 billion, would be rescheduled.

Of total Latin American indebtedness, to the amount of $360 billion or more:

- Brazil accounts for $100 billion
- Mexico for almost $90 billion
- Argentina for $50 billion
- and Venezuela for $35 billion.

Three hundred and sixty billion dollars means $45 billion a year in bank interest. Rescheduling has resulted in additional fees and harsh conditions on the budgetary policy of the countries concerned and on the distribution of the burden of the crisis. As a rule, decisions have been made at the expense of the poorer sections of society, those with a low standard of living, and those who need public support or have no kind of access to any sources of relief – higher bread prices then just mean more hunger.

One may ask how such a mountain of debt, with all its consequences, could have come into being. The answer is only partially provided by miscalculations, as in the projected sales and price of oil, and by mismanagement on the part of the debtor countries, which could of course be noted as well. But when loans are taken up and applications made and granted for credit, there is a double responsibility: responsibility on the part of the lender as well as the borrower. In minimizing that responsibility, some speak of 'incorrect estimates of the scope for debt'. It is seldom admitted that the banks themselves indulged in an orgy of credit offers.

The Latin Americans are accused of having allowed a severe flight of capital to aggravate their problems. In 1984 flight capital amounted to over a third of their outstanding foreign debts. However, we should not forget that liquid capital is basically inclined to stray. Why should it show national responsibility for which there is little or no incentive in a given region, and when, moreover, the corresponding sense of responsibility is highly underdeveloped . . .?

Capital urgently needed in Europe is at present flowing out as well, and into the USA, complying with none but economic incentives: higher interest rates and greater security. The United States' high expenditure on armaments is known to be extensively financed by budget deficits – as at the time of the Vietnam War – which in turn send interest rates up, with the result that the developing countries, particularly the newly industrializing countries, who have gone into debt on a basis of variable interest, are unexpectedly encumbered to the tune of several billion dollars more.

At the meeting of the IMF in the autumn of 1984, even leading figures in the management of the World Bank rejected Washington's thesis that activity set off in the wake of the US budget deficit compensated for the major part of the burden of high interest, and the Third World must invest more resources and labour in exports. The reports of the IMF itself remark critically upon the fact that the mighty United States is solving its problems at other people's expense, importing capital which weaker countries need for their development.

In the USA itself, well-known economists are speaking out, expressing their concern at seeing their country well on the way to becoming the biggest debtor nation of all. Government experts expect a record budget deficit of $210 billion for 1985 (it was $175 billion in the financial year 1984). Another rise in interest rates is not impossible.

Experts dispute the question of whether the credit crisis has come about because of inadequate regulation of financial policy on the international markets, or whether the credit business has burst out of the framework which objectively should contain it. Why not assume a combination of both factors? In any case, there can be no doubt that in essence we are dealing with a decline in economic activity rather than the covering of credit as shown by the books. It is no contradiction that the excessive amount of debt worldwide must be reduced if the steep rise in interest rates is to be counteracted.

Future economic development had certainly been wrongly estimated in all countries, and in consequence, erroneous dispositions had been made. Just as certainly, there is a capital flight based on rules of conduct other than that of national responsibility. Those who are constantly demanding performance speculate on interest rates and through speculative capital movements. In any event, responsibility for the extent of the credit crisis should not be sought solely in the debtors.

2. A Blood Transfusion from the Sick to the Healthy

Over the last few years, debtor countries have become capital exporters – an absurd situation. An extensive net capital transfer from poorer countries to rich countries has set in, to a large extent to the private banks, improving their balance sheets. Debtors have had to borrow more money to service their debts with those same banks. Even in the USA, there has been talk of a 'perverse transfer of money away from the poor'. Another suggested metaphor was a 'blood transfusion from the sick to the healthy', and there are object lessons to show us the accuracy of that.

To take the case of Mexico: the second debt rescheduling, for a period of 14 years, will amount to *one and a half* times the original debt, i.e. $130 billion. At a meeting with government representatives in Mexico City, I asked if it was true that parts of the first rescheduling had cost 30 per cent in interest and fees. Yes, I was told, that might well be so.

We thus see circumstances such as the following arise:

- Latin America's foreign debts of $360 billion, with an interest rate in real terms of 'only' 10 per cent, mean that over $40 billion end up annually in New York, London and Frankfurt. In fact the Latin Americans recorded a negative net transfer of capital of $55 billion in 1984.
- When US interest on long-term loans rose by another 3 per cent in early 1984, the debts of Latin America instantly shot up by another $5 billion.
- The sum paid out by the countries of Latin America in 1983–84 in interest on their foreign debts corresponded to about 50 per cent of their export earnings.

The debtor countries have thus been obliged, and still are, to meet their interest payments with an excessive proportion of their export earnings. With the inclusion of redemption rates, the total came to over 100 per cent for some individual countries. The situation is becoming intolerable:

- In Brazil, the proportion of export earnings required to service interest on debts rose from 24 to over 40 per cent between 1978 and 1983.
- In Argentina, it rose from less than 10 per cent to 57 per cent of export earnings. (By now, if there had been no rescheduling, four years' export earnings would be needed for one year's servicing of Argentina's debts.)
- Mexico, an oil-producing country, will have to spend half its export earnings servicing its debts over the next few years – and that is after rescheduling.
- Peru would have had to employ 80 per cent of its export earnings in 1984 to meet its obligations. The country has temporarily relieved its burdens by refinancing and by leaving commitments unmet.
- Even in a small Central American state like Costa Rica, servicing its debts accounts for 50 per cent and in Panama for 40 per cent of export earnings.
- In the Dominican Republic, the debt service ratio amounted to a third of export earnings at the end of 1982, and it has since risen.

Rescheduling programmes generally are agreed only under pressure. Social consequences are disregarded. However, even in German banking and European economic circles, reference is sometimes made to the 'limits of political and social tolerance' which might be reached if financial rehabilitation measures agreed upon with IMF were to be put through. Even some politicians of a conservative tendency have pointed out that IMF would be inviting social and political unrest if it turned the screw too tight in the debtor countries and went so far as to endanger the feeding of their people.

These are not just theoretical considerations any more. Social unrest resulting from steep price rises in basic foodstuffs – as occurred in 1984 in the Dominican Republic, Mexico, Brazil, Argentina, Bolivia and Chile – may have been a portent of more serious protests to come. People have rebelled against the deterioration in elementary living conditions in other parts of the world too: in Tunisia, Morocco and Egypt on one hand, in the Philippines on the other.

It has become fashionable to make the International Monetary Fund an international scapegoat. I have serious reservations about it myself – they are set out in detail in our two reports – but I would not like to be a party to bringing criticism to bear in the wrong quarters. For neither the Monetary Fund nor the World Bank are institutions operating in a void. They do what the governments of their most important and vociferous member countries tell them to do, or what the member countries will allow to pass without contradicting. Those who complain of IMF or the World Bank should really direct their complaints to those governments who, in the last resort, have the say in decision-making.

In our two reports, my colleagues and I suggested ways in which these international institutions could be reformed. I have already mentioned the initial reactions of leading governments: either none at all or unfavourable. Only under the pressure of intensifying crisis does such an attitude slowly, very slowly, seem to be changing.

There is no doubt that in many respects IMF has played an impressive part. Its French managing director, with capable and sometimes too zealous colleagues from many countries, has performed Herculean labours, 'case by case', and not just during the Mexican crisis; commercial banks and international organizations, governments and central banks have all had to be brought together, transitional solutions have had to be found to avert worse developments. The people who work for the institution are authoritative experts, though they may have a rather conservative outlook and perhaps not enough insight into social needs. The waste of funds on military purposes is generally excluded from their discussions and statements, because many governments do not openly set out the relevant expenditure in their budgets, or are not ready to discuss the issue of national security with IMF. However, IMF itself, if often without public knowledge, has regularly endeavoured to obtain the relevant figures and information and not leave the subject unconsidered because of economic effects on the appropriate economic policy.

It is unrealistic to reject IMF conditionality in principle. However, it *must* be asked why conditions have not also been laid down for the industrial and other rich countries. The immediate answer is: conditions are part of an agreement made with IMF for balance of payments support, and only governments in difficulties will be concluding such stand-by agreements. But it is interesting and instructive to note that the tone of criticism of IMF was just the same, say, in Italy and Great Britain – at any rate at the time when those European countries were dependent on the help of the Monetary Fund and needed a stand-by agreement. Is such a thing quite out of the question in the case of the USA?

Those affected ask, rightly, why one cannot refrain from measures which mean economic contraction, fall most heavily on the poorer sections of society, and neglect long-term development. One might go further and ask: why not allow the developing countries too to practise whatever kind of mixed economy is suited to them instead of imposing ideological as well as material conditions? The answer is ready to hand. It is a question of whose word bears weight where. But that itself shows why the developing countries should have more of a say where decisions concerning them are made.

My criticism is thus mainly addressed not to IMF as such, but to the policy it pursues, which is decided by leading industrial states, in particular the USA. The USA stands in the way of IMF's ability to obtain more funds, under defensible conditions and less restrictions. The Fund lets the great powers off lightly, contenting itself with warily academic comments on high interest rates. Those who speak for Europe do not improve matters, since they either think their supposed national advantage more important, failing to recognize their international political responsibility, or because they have opted for a permanent fear of their great friend.

It would be wrong to suppose that these problems and dangers are not perceived in the United States as well. They often find public expression there, in Congress as well as the more serious sections of the press. When the Latin American debt crisis was looming, there was no lack of civil servants in the Treasury Department in Washington, if not at the very highest, politically occupied level, who issued warnings and made constructive suggestions. But they got as little of a hearing as those who tried to explain the character of the Central American revolutionary movements. Those who attempted to explain the Cuban revolution at the end of the Fifties had also found that their words fell on deaf ears, and the same thing had happened to those repudiated a decade earlier because they advocated a reasonable policy towards China.

Important as Latin America is, however, we should not overlook the fact that there are now Asian countries which are fundamentally no more solvent, to say nothing of most of the African countries. Referring to the latter, de Larosière, Managing Director of IMF, has said: 'This escalation of debt must not continue.'

Unfortunately, however, it seems that the rule applying to private debtors also applies, on a large scale, to states: if someone owes £1,000, that is his problem; if he owes £100,000, it is his bank's. Highly reputable financial journals have thus written, correctly, of the 'other' or 'forgotten' debt crisis, when referring to the smaller and poorer developing countries. These countries are neglected because their debts make up only a small part of the debt mountain, and because they generally have little to offer economically. Their people suffer no less from the consequences.

We may remember the wry joke about exploitation: if IMF comes along, things are bad; if it doesn't come along at all, or only late in the day, things are even worse.

In the long run, we shall not master this global crisis by

patching up holes here, there, and everywhere, but by making coordinated international efforts to begin reducing the size of the debt mountain, and taking the requisite reform of the international monetary and financial system seriously.

3. *Latin America: Crisis versus Democracy*

In the autumn of 1984, on a visit to a number of Latin American countries I was able to form an idea of the way the democratization process is going there, in the face of debt crises and severe economic difficulties. Both the pressing economic problems, and the clear drift away from military dictatorship and towards democracy, were more marked than I had realized from a distance.

I was well aware that several of those countries had made considerable economic progress in the Sixties and Seventies, though they were very far from having achieved social equality. But now constitutional issues topped the agenda:

- In Argentina, the new democratic order made its breakthrough with the election of President Raúl Alfonsín at the end of 1983. That election had repercussions on the whole continent, and symbolic significance too. However, we heard anxious questions: could the democracy expect support in good time, or would it come too late? That question has yet to be answered.
- In the vast country of Brazil too, the military dictators had shown their economic incompetence, thus preparing the way for the election of a civilian President, Tancredo Neves. He died before he could take office, but the interim coalition seemed to be up to its democratic task.
- I had met representatives of the Uruguayan democratic opposition when attending a conference in Rio. One of them, Julio M. Sanguinetti, was elected President shortly afterwards. The military judged it advisable to go back to their barracks.
- Peru was preparing for the democratic change by holding elections – for the first time in years. Although civil war was raging in parts of the country, the young Social Democrat

leader Alan García was able to take over as President, without further military intervention. He is pursuing a demanding programme of rural renewal and internal pacification.

- In Cartagena in Colombia, President Belisario Betancur – a conservative of an idiosyncratic nature, having been, as he himself says, 'baptized with reddish water' – told me how he was getting guerrilla fighters who had spent years in the forests to come to the negotiating table. When Betancur speaks of the 'objective agents' of subversion, he means malnutrition and unemployment, and the shortage of schools and hospitals.

- Chile is having particular difficulty in overcoming military dictatorship. One of the most moving experiences of my journey was the moment when the leaders of the Chilean opposition came to the airport during our stopover at Santiago; on the plane, a Chilean industrialist told me that he personally, like the trade unionists, was in favour of joint attempts at a new democracy.

Despite all these impressive experiences, however, the democratic process in Latin America is still at risk. Not just because of the pressing problems of foreign trade and finance, but on account of gross economic and social inequalities within those countries too. In Argentina, there was talk of inflation of the order of several hundred per cent (in March 1985, 800 per cent was the figure mentioned). Data from Brazil spoke of 200 per cent inflation, and the Peruvian figure was 125. In Bolivia, over 2,000 per cent was registered. The establishing of these approximate values is no doubt connected with the method of calculating them. President Alfonsín mentioned the total collapse of the German currency after the First World War, which I myself had witnessed as a child. Where was the present situation leading? And were we in the West going to help the new democracy or wait to lay wreaths on its grave? Another of the Presidents likened the situation to the painful experience of undergoing an operation without anaesthetic. And indeed, the outlook for the democrats of those countries is not particularly good, hampered as they are by the crippling debt service.

An extremely unjust distribution of income, inadequate food supplies, lack of social facilities, also of schools for the children of the poorer classes, are typical of the situation as a whole, with a generally low standard of living of a great majority of the population. It is obvious that there will be a struggle not just for the existence of political democracy, but for its economic basis and social orientation, for a new meaning to independence.

'More and more people have less and less to eat,' was the way a Brazilian bishop summed up the situation. While great quantities of food are destined for export, millions of Brazilians are mal-nourished. Wages in real terms have sunk below the 1970 level. The infant mortality rate has risen again, particularly in the north-east of that vast country. When Leonel Brizola, governor of the state of Rio de Janeiro, took office in 1982, 700,000 children had no schooling. Within two years, he told me, he was able to halve that number; one method he employed was the introduc-tion of a school meals service.

Before the Second World War Argentina used to be compared with Canada, just as Uruguay was called the Switzerland of South America. Argentina is still considered a newly industrializing country, but like Uruguay can display alarming instances of the reverse of development. Today, and without any population explosion, those countries suffer not just from the consequences of dictatorship and the failings of the world economy, but to a considerable degree from self-inflicted and practically chaotic economic and financial conditions, high unemployment and ex-orbitant prices. The standard of living has sunk by 30 to 40 per cent since 1975.

In Mexico, wages in real terms dropped by 30 per cent in the two years after the debt débâcles of 1982; the proportion of unemployed and underemployed is estimated at almost 50 per cent.

In Peru, the President of the Central Bank observed: 'Our per capita income has dropped to its 1965 level.' Forty per cent of the population is described as undernourished. Export earnings from agrarian products have dropped even more sharply than those from mineral commodities.

In Colombia, the usual problems of the continent are inten-sified by the slow, and indeed in the short term imperceptible, progress being made in fighting the unwholesome influence of the drugs Mafia; that destructive factor looms even larger in Bolivia.

Even in Venezuela, distinguished by large revenues from oil and less population pressure, and on the whole better off than most countries of the South American continent, 20 per cent unemployment is presumed to exist, with a percentage twice that figure in the capital. None the less, my friend Carlos Andres Perez, former President of Venezuela, who accompanied me on an important part of my Latin American journey, remains as optimistic as ever about his continent's future.

He is not the only one to believe that the Latin Americans are incorrectly classified. They think of themselves as part of the Third World, but do not want to be entirely absorbed by it. The cultural heritage of Spain and Portugal, ancient Indian culture, modern American and European influences are all in a process of new amalgamation. Distrust of both superpowers is strong. So is the feeling of being neglected by Europe. There is no doubt that Europeans could do much good, and play a much larger part in Latin America than they do at present.

It would be a mistake, one to which many in the region are prone, to seek the causes of their troubles only outside themselves. In Latin America more than anywhere, the upper stratum of society bears a large share of responsibility for the existing misery suffered elsewhere. (As the Pope has said: 'The increasing wealth of a few stands beside the increasing misery of the masses.') If one is talking of exploitation, one cannot very well overlook the exploitation in the countries themselves. Crisis and democracy – it is a subject which cannot just be shifted on to the agenda of international conferences.

And incidentally, the member of a foreign delegation – or the visiting economist, or the prosperous tourist – will see little of what concerns and oppresses the ordinary people of the continent unless he or she takes a positive interest in it. Such visitors are accommodated in first-class hotels, welcomed into elegant offices and fine houses, and eat in good restaurants. Unless one is careful, one is in danger of altogether missing the reality of the country visited, particularly on a short stay in a Latin American country.

To be frank: anyone who arrives at the international airport in Rio or São Paulo, Mexico City or Buenos Aires, who is driven through office and business districts and spends a few days at a conference centre, must be careful that the long shadows cast by the country in which he is staying do not escape his notice. The same applies to Cairo and Delhi, Djakarta and Kuala Lumpur as to the capital cities of Latin America. If you see the considerable prosperity, sometimes the great luxury of the economic élite of society, and frequently of the political élite as well, you will find yourself wondering if you are really in a poor country after all.

In many cases, poor countries are those which, objectively speaking, are rich. The privileged, typically, are strikingly opulent; the lot of the poverty-stricken masses is unhappy, indeed desperate. Only the unobservant will fail to take in the whole of the truth around them.

4. *Alternatives?*

At the beginning of the Seventies the international monetary system was dismantled when it ought to have been renovated. The visible sign of financial instability came with the suspension of the convertibility at a fixed rate of the dollar into gold. The Eurodollar market was blown up to twice the official currency reserves, chiefly as a result of the oil crisis. The international financial system became subject to increasing privatization, while the developing countries had inadequate opportunities of obtaining finance. When loans were not repaid, banks were happy enough to be able to renew them and roll them over, to good advantage, since interest rates were rising.

However, the industrial states, led by the USA, had gone so far down the road of debt themselves that the consequences could not be long in coming. Even rather conservative Americans spoke openly of the defects of the international monetary system; many Europeans were no longer afraid to say that the United States did not live up to the responsibility imposed upon it by the role of the dollar. Some of the proposals we made five years ago were taken more seriously now. The governments of Europe found themselves required by the European parliamentary assemblies to aim to create an international reserve currency, taking the needs of the poorest countries into account. Basically, there are three main points at issue:

- First, can IMF be strengthened and reformed so that it assumes at least partially the role of a global central bank, and if so how? It would mean extending the role of Special Drawing Rights and altering the voting system in favour of the developing countries.

- Secondly, can the World Bank be put in a position to expand its annual volume of lending considerably, and ensure that the developing countries have more of a say? A word of caution: the Indian who graduated from Harvard or the Chilean who graduated from Chicago, whose family is not exactly poverty-stricken, and who has not overcome his own class-consciousness, is in no way a 'better' choice as colleague than an American or European, Japanese or Australian from a similar background. Nationality alone says little. (IDA, a subject on which I have already expressed my opinion, must also be seen as a part of the World Bank. So must IFC, the International Finance Corporation, which encourages private investment in developing countries by means of direct participation. The various regional development banks work in a similar way, and their activities deserve positive interest, though their role is not specifically elucidated here.)

- Thirdly, what should the nature of an international conference be to determine urgent issues of money, finance, and general economic matters?

Indira Gandhi had asked experts from the non-aligned countries to draw up the report which came out in the summer of 1984: it employed weighty if not particularly new arguments to set out the objections to an 'adjustment' providing neither employment nor significant growth. A conference with universal participation, planned for the autumn of 1985, was to take place in the context of 'directions in development policies', aiming for resolutions based on consensus; the preparations were to be made by a representative group from both industrial and developing countries, with the support of IMF, the World Bank and UNCTAD.

After Indira Gandhi's assassination, it turned out that more time was needed to realize these plans. But I am sure that her ideas will not be forgotten. Several factors indicate that we shall not master crises in the long term by dealing with them case by case. I would like to mention a few recent developments.

The resources of IMF *have* been stocked up considerably in recent years, but the governments whose word carries weight in the Fund do not want their *status quo* disturbed where Special Drawing Rights are concerned. Five years ago, we suggested a well-founded increase of $100 billion. American experts advocated just under half that amount, moderate European experts recommended an annual, quantitatively limited SDR allocation. They saw the solution as the combination of a smaller burden of interest with more – responsibly secured – new money.

The Western economic summits in London, 1984, and Bonn, 1985, were non-events so far as the debt crisis was concerned. The participants did rouse themselves to encourage the banks to make rescheduling agreements for periods of several years 'in suitable cases and in the presence of corresponding progress in adjustment'. At the same time, the governments declared themselves ready to negotiate rescheduling of official government loans. The progress made in 'adjustment' by the debtor countries was to be rewarded with more favourable conditions. Some governments did not agree with this excessively cautious approach. France wanted the creation of three additional tranches of $15 billion SDRs each.

The French representative at the United Nations said, in the autumn of 1984, that the world economic system must become less complex and should be marked by stability, and hence it needed restructuring. In the long term, steps must be taken to lay the foundations of genuine international currency reform; besides the dollar, the yen and the West European ECU (European Currency Unit) should be central factors in this future system. I regret that these French initiatives did not get support at least from the German Federal government.

Meanwhile experienced critics outside government circles have spoken out. Karl Schiller, for instance, reminded us of the old experience that as a general rule, a compromise settlement is preferable to the threat of insolvency. One of the big Swiss bankers said publicly and frankly that the banks must know they would not get back the money they had lent, and should be content with a moderate yield of interest. Other European bankers said that long-term rescheduling was better than short-term rescheduling whose conditions the countries concerned could not live up to. Finally, the head of the German Bundesbank asked for the phase of crisis management to be followed by a phase of longer-term consolidation, 'even if there were to be some uncomfortable consequences for the participating banks' profit and loss accounts'. In the USA, Henry Kissinger said that anyone relying on the present system of debt negotiations might just as well be playing Russian roulette. Declining to repay loans was no longer dismissed as immoral.

Meanwhile, the Latin American debtor countries had become impatient, and were speaking of financial colonialism and saying that South America must emancipate herself from foreign rule imposed by international financial circles. They wanted to negotiate only at a high political level. In practice, however, they had to climb down; the structural factors were altogether too powerful – or still too powerful. I can understand how the phrase 'imperialism through credit' arose.

At various meetings, in Quito, Cartagena, and Mar del Plata, eleven Latin American countries had agreed in principle on a common front to be presented to the creditor countries. Some of them talked grandly, speaking of landmarks along the road of concerted action against the industrial countries. But in practice, things looked different; talks on rescheduling continued as before between the individual debtor countries and their creditors, with either more or less attention being paid to their agreed debtors' principles.

Responsible people have said to me in conversation that here again it cannot be just a matter of distinguishing between multilateral rhetoric and bilateral pragmatism, closely as that would correspond to the facts. It is much more important, they say, to interpret the signs of the times correctly: the larger countries saw their agreements as a first step towards joint action by the Latin American family, which had met without the leadership of Washington for the first time, 150 years after independence. In that way, initiatives like those of Quito, Cartagena and Mar del Plata represented great progress.

There is a general intention of removing negotiations on rescheduling from the present technical level to a high political level, and conducting the discussion in the larger context of international economic relations, and paying particular attention to trade issues as well. The agreement made at the annual meeting of IMF and the World Bank in the autumn of 1984 to conduct such talks in the framework of the Development Committee – an important coordinating committee between the Fund and the Bank, if not at the highest level – was apparently not a large enough step.

When Tancredo Neves was elected President of Brazil, he ruled out the possibility of a moratorium on his country's debts. He wanted to start new negotiations on unreasonable conditions of repayment, while for the time being prohibiting the taking up of more loans from US banks. Only passing mention was made of a 'dangerous' cartel of debtor countries. (President Nyerere, who advised his African colleagues not to service their debts as a means of exerting pressure, was not representative in this respect.) Mexico's President de la Madrid declared himself in favour of a 'pragmatic dialogue', and emphasized the 'great variety of problems and positions' within the Third World. All governments were under pressure, but some less so than others. They all drew attention, he said, to their own particular circumstances, they almost all disclaimed the existence in the immediate future of any real alternative to the adjustments imposed on them and the resulting interim provisions. South America itself had only the beginnings of a regional mechanism with whose help effective preparations could be made for concerted action. If the process of coordination were accelerated during the current crisis, that, he said, could only be helpful to all concerned, including the creditor countries.

In October 1984, at a conference in Rio de Janeiro – Governor Brizola had invited the Socialist International – ideas for the management of the debt crisis emerged, which I put forward for discussion at the various stages of my subsequent Latin American journey, and for which I won the agreement of those concerned. They were as follows:

- a moratorium on debts; in addition, a waiving of the debts of the poorest countries;
- a lowering of interest rates, to be linked to the simultaneous

establishment of an upper ceiling; to the surprise of many, the Chairman of the Federal Reserve Bank of the United States himself also spoke of a 'cap on interest rates';

- the introduction of a 'social clause'. This would ensure that the programme of adjustment did not lower the standard of living of the poorest classes unreasonably; instead, the minimum acceptable living standard should be taken as a firm criterion;
- I would add here that an international conference on debts may well become unavoidable.

We shall have to wait and see when and how all these points are eventually taken up. I have already said that I think a second Bretton Woods is required. And one can only hope that those politicians chiefly responsible will apply themselves to the matter in time; for there are plenty of technical proposals, and in the long term experts are inclined to divide into two camps of equal strength: one camp puts forward all possible reasons for a given proposal, the other rejects it for reasons that sound equally plausible. But if one listens only to one camp or the other, one gets nowhere.

5. *Unremitting Trade War*

One of the many disappointments of 1984 was the failure of the UNIDO conference in Vienna. UNIDO (the United Nations Industrial Development Organization) was created in 1966 to promote industrial development of the Third World. In 1975, at a conference in Lima, it was still being estimated that the developing countries would command a quarter of global industrial production in the year 2000. In 1984 they had 12 per cent of it, and it was not thought likely that they would reach over 18 per cent by the turn of the century. The Vienna conference did not come up to expectations.

At that conference, the USA stated that in allocating development aid, they would give preference to countries with a free market economy. It is still not clear how that criterion is to be established, or to whose advantage such dogmatism is supposed to be. In several of the countries closely associated with the USA, and of which they approve – such as South Korea – a high degree of state control of the economy is practised. And when the United States and their principal European allies urge IMF to impose stringent conditions, they are not as a general rule aiming at free enterprise initiative but at practising greater government control in whatever country is concerned.

There is no doubt that the developing countries' access to the markets of the industrial countries is obstructed by the same groups that like to talk of free market economy and free world trade. At the annual GATT meeting at the end of 1984, it was pointed out from the chair that despite some increase in the volume of world trade, the climate of international trade relations had deteriorated; the growth of world trade, which could be attributed to the prevailing trend of economic activity in Japan and the USA, had been accompanied by a rise in protectionism. Those chiefly affected were the developing countries.

A clear trend away from multilateral free trade and towards the bilateral, controlled exchange of goods may be observed globally. There is talk of a 'fragmentation' of markets, creating insecurity in the economy and slowing down capital investments outside the USA.

The assurances given by many governments are highly disingenuous. Sixty per cent of world trade is transacted under 'non-free' conditions. Of the total industrial products consumed in the USA and the EEC, over 30 per cent are now affected by protectionist measures; a few years ago, it was about 20 per cent.

When a new round of international trade negotiations was envisaged in the spring of 1985, first in the OECD and then at the world economic summit in Bonn, there was no lack of warning voices to be heard from those who thought a link between trade and *monetary* issues was imperative. This connection is of particular interest to many developing countries.

In the first half of the Eighties, the developing countries were affected more than anyone by an increase in protectionist measures, particularly in textiles and clothing, steel, and agricultural products. UNCTAD registered no less than 21,000 cases in which 'non-tariff' barriers (i.e. barriers other than customs duties) had been employed – guerrilla warfare in trade policy, with permanent effects.

The tendency to short-sighted protectionism is spreading, while on the other hand the division of production – or chain production – plays an ever-increasing part in global economic cooperation, from footwear to car manufacture. The role of the multinational corporations is seen again here. To give a bizarre example: 95 per cent of all baseball bats, as used in America, come from Japan. First the hides of American cattle are sent to Brazil for tanning, then they go on to Japan to cover the baseball bats.

> With the restrictions and trade barriers of recent years, we have seen the shifting and interlocking of whole branches of industry between country and continent. Here are some examples (taken from John Naisbitt, *Megatrends*):
> - Singapore comes in second place, just behind the USA, for orders for building offshore oil-rigs;
> - Hong Kong and Taiwan are dropping out of the production of textiles and simple electrical goods in order to concentrate more intensively on computer technology;
> - South Korea is challenging Japan's dominance in home electronics;
> - The People's Republic of China, which concentrated on the export of commodities in the Seventies, is moving into the production and export of products of light industry, textiles, baskets, bicycles, radio and television sets.

Despite enormous shifts, it is not yet clear what opportunities will be offered to developing countries in the markets of industrial countries in the years ahead. The concept of an international society of unrestricted competition was shaken when competition itself was overcome in a number of branches of industry; multinational corporations and governments had made ample use of their opportunities. Exchange between the fundamentally unequal, in any case, entails its own grave problems, let alone the built-in handicaps in any race where a man with one leg is competing against a man with two.

As I have mentioned, the Allies' postwar planning envisaged an international Trade Organization (ITO). When nothing came of this, GATT, the General Agreement on Tariffs and Trade, became the most important liberator of world trade. Although GATT provides for the protection of a country's domestic economy exclusively by means of tariffs, and not without consultation, precisely the opposite has occurred in an increasing number of cases over the years, particularly in recent times. Trade restrictions are constantly supplementing or succeeding one another, and there are many cases of sudden action being taken, instead of serious efforts to reach understanding. Job losses in the industrial states as the result of imports from the South have in fact been less than was at first expected, while on the other hand the potentially growing significance of exports to Third World countries has been underestimated. Those who would reduce the export incomes of the newly industrializing countries should, however, be aware that they are simultaneously reducing the ability of those countries to buy capital goods.

With a view to comprehensive international trade organization my Commission recommended:

- creating *one* organization, which would incorporate both GATT and UNCTAD;
- protecting, for a certain period, endangered regions or branches of the economy, while paying serious attention to those structural adjustments necessary as a result of the international division of labour;
- regarding the protection of domestic markets in developing countries as entirely legitimate;
- giving strong support to increased South–South cooperation (and we have seen remarkable progress made in this area);
- recognizing the dangers which are the inevitable consequence of the further spread of narrow-minded protectionism.

In the American debate, too, those with international experience have suggested the kind of principles for necessary adjustments for which one should aim. If relatively free trade is to function, governments would have to overcome 'full laissez-faire'. This judgment has realism and honesty on its side, and so do those who now admit that they do after all recognize the advantage of an assured supply of raw materials at predictable prices.

However, some of the emotional attacks on European agrarian

policy are full of inconsistencies. I am one of the critics of the excesses of that policy, and have been for some time. I think they are also to be deplored and resisted from the angle of development policy. However, one cannot see the justification for American polemic against European subsidies if it is in fact only a matter of *who* is doing the subsidizing, and by *how much*. (In the USA, subsidies to farmers are more per head than in the EEC – a French friend of mine spoke of 'wallowing in the most consummate form of hypocrisy'.)

The agricultural policy of the European Community *does* need extensive revision. In the process, the interests of a constructive development policy must come into their own. By the way, it is only right that the EEC should not allow itself to discriminate in its industrial and research policy.

As for the multinational or transnational corporations, the negotiations in progress since 1977 over an international code of conduct have come to a halt; no agreement is in sight.

These were the recommendations formulated by my Commission:

- With regard to foreign investments, transfer of technology, repatriation of profits, royalties and dividends: reciprocal obligations on the part of host and home countries.
- With regard to activities of transnational corporations in matters such as ethical behaviour, disclosure of information, restrictive business practices and labour standards: legislation coordinated between home and host countries to regulate them.
- In matters of tax policy and the monitoring of transfer pricing: intergovernmental cooperation.
- With regard to fiscal and other incentives between developing countries in which transnational or multinational corporations are active: harmonization.

Over the last few years it has become even clearer what the transnational corporations represent. They control a third of world production, and transact 40 per cent of world trade between them. In certain sectors, particularly commodities, up to 90 per cent of the trade is in their hands. Over the last two

decades, their activity has grown twice as fast as world production and world trade. Their profits in developing countries are on
average twice as high as 'at home' in the industrial states. The
multinationals are using their chances as best they can. Criticism
should be levelled principally at the backwardness that marks the
policies of many governments.

6. Natural Resources on the Sea-Bed

A disappointment in my own country was the refusal of its
government in 1984 to sign the Law of the Sea Convention, which
had come into existence two years earlier after very lengthy
negotiations, and was perhaps the most important international
treaty since the United Nations Charter.

When my Commission met in Ottawa at the end of 1982, and
were putting the finishing touches to our second Report, we were
visited by Elisabeth Mann-Borghese, Thomas Mann's daughter.
She told us of the results of the work in which she, as an authority,
had had a large share since 1958. Our Commission firmly believed that it was 'clearly in the interests of all nations to sign this
Convention'. One hundred and nineteen states had agreed to the
draft drawn up in Jamaica. The Convention was signed by 158
states and groups of states in 1984, though ratified by only a few.
Among the overwhelming majority of the community of states
that declared themselves in favour of this important treaty are
almost all Third World countries, China, Japan, the Soviet Union
and almost all European countries. The USA, which had once set
the initiative in motion, was now simply opposed to it – influenced by the special interest of its private mining corporations
in the future mining of the sea-bed – and secured the allegiance of
the United Kingdom, the Federal Republic of Germany, and
Israel.

I was very sorry to see the Bonn government, not for the first
time, yielding so far to American intervention as to run the risk of
isolating itself. An independent assessment of our interests in
terms of foreign and economic policy would have led to a
different view. German interests do not automatically coincide

with those currently supported by the United States, particularly over the Law of the Sea, and not only because, unlike the USA, Germany is neither a world power nor the possessor of a large seaboard. Germany also lost its chance of making Hamburg the headquarters of the International Court of the Law of the Sea.

The Law of the Sea Convention is concerned with:
- regulating seafaring and fishing rights; and no one could expect that that might do away with the objective advantage of states with large seaboards;
- the demarcation of territorial and economic zones at sea (to which the same applies);
- measures against the contamination of the seas and the decimation of marine fauna;
- basic regulations for scientific and technical cooperation between North and South;
- regulations for deep-sea mining, although this will hardly be a very important factor before the year 2000.

The issue disputed most is the last point: under what conditions are so-called manganese nodules to be mined? Besides manganese, these contain cobalt, copper and nickel, and are found in large quantities on the sea-bed. The international treaty was to turn just these natural resources – a 'common inheritance of mankind' – to good account for all nations jointly, under the supervision of an international authority. The professional expertise of the few industrial states active in this area and in a position to build the expensive plant needed was to have been made available to the developing countries.

The objection raised was to the 'regulatory' powers of the envisaged authority, which it was supposed would offend the order principles of the free market economy. The fact was that certain large companies did not want to subscribe to a system of international law. Behind the principles of political order for which support is claimed, to impress the public, there lies a colonialist notion of the first law – also a kind of gold-digger's mentality, for which, however, there are no real grounds.

This is an area in which judicious international control is called for. And I would continue to plead for a good part of that common heritage of mankind to be freed for purposes of economic development.

The dispute over the Law of the Sea Convention is one proof among others of the dire straits in which multilateralism finds itself – and the present belief of many developing countries that they will do better if they concentrate on bilateral relations is certainly a contributing factor. Those who have long striven for the interests of such countries to be reconciled with those of the industrial countries are all the more discouraged.

7. A New Marshall Plan?

After the Second World War, the American Marshall Plan played a considerable part in helping Western Europe to get on its feet again; Stalin would not permit an extension of economic aid into his new sphere of influence. The United States made sacrifices, but they also got something in return. Over the last few years, it has repeatedly been asked whether the basic concepts of the plan named after Secretary of State (and former General) George Marshall could not be applied to the relation between industrial and developing countries.

Nor is the question unreasonable. A simple equation cannot, of course, be made. The existence in Europe of an industrial basis, preserved despite all the destruction, and of a large, experienced labour force, represented conditions there which are not present in large parts of the Third World.

My friends in the German Parliament took the idea as a starting point when they proposed a 'Third World Future Programme' in the middle of 1984. The introduction to their proposal says: 'The future of the Third World is not chiefly determined by outside aid. Rather, it is crucially dependent on the emergence of a more just economic and social order for the world as a whole.' The Future Programme was not, said the proposal, merely a humane requirement: 'It is not only based on the historical co-responsibility of the industrial nations; it is also in their own interests.'

After 1945, the Marshall Plan provided the impetus for the reconstruction of Europe and contributed to the recovery of the world economy. Today we need to make a similarly great effort to combat hunger and disease, the exploitation and destruction of the natural environment, the waste of energy and raw materials, ignorance and unemployment in the Third World: 'However, it cannot, as with the Marshall Plan, be a case of involving the developing countries in the political and economic system of the industrial states. What is required, rather, is global cooperation corresponding to the cultural and social identity and the political and economic independent responsibility of the developing countries.'

The basic principles of such a programme are simple: they consist of taking concrete action to bring about the necessary reduction in global expenditure on armaments and the use of the resources thus saved for the development of the Third World. But the aim of such a 'Third World Future Programme' goes beyond the call for funds to be diverted from military expenditure. It demands a new approach to international cooperation world-wide, for only thus would the anticipated resource transfer to the developing countries be possible at all. And an essential part of this approach is better cooperation between East and West. This is a return to the 'philosophy' behind our two reports: the peoples of the world have no choice but to secure their survival together. That can happen only if world peace is secured. And that requires the economic and social development of the Third World.

An emergency programme forms the nucleus of the project I am describing. Overcoming the international debt crisis will have a central part to play in the economic future of many countries not just in the Third World, but among the industrial nations too. A 'Third World' special programme cannot stop there. There are close connections here with the proposals of the Brandt Commission, since, as we said, 'the world cannot wait for the longer-term measures before embarking on an immediate action programme for the next five years to avert the most serious dangers, an interlocking programme which will require undertakings by all parties, and also bring benefits to all'.

Four large areas fell within the scope of the emergency programme as set out in our report in 1980:

First, a large-scale transfer of resources to developing countries, to be brought about by the provision of:

- aid for the poorest regions, which are worst affected by economic crises,
- aid for middle-income countries, by providing finance for their debts and deficits.

Second, an international energy strategy, to consist of:

- regular supplies of oil,
- predictable and gradual price rises,
- the development of sources of alternative and renewable energy.

Third, a global food programme, its aims being:

- increased production of food, with international assistance, especially in the Third World itself,
- regular food supplies, including increased emergency aid,
- a system for long-term international food security.

Fourth, the introduction of major reforms of the international economic system, to be achieved by:

- taking steps towards an effective international monetary and financial system in such a way that all could participate with equal rights,
- accelerating efforts to improve the developing countries' conditions of trade in commodities and manufactured products.

The 'Third World Future Programme' concentrates on the essential areas of:

- decreasing the burden of debt on the poorest countries,
- ensuring the satisfaction of basic needs, particularly through increased food production in the developing countries themselves,
- promoting trade and improved conditions of trade for those countries.

Responsibility for use of resources and control over such use could lie with a new international committee, North and South having equal representation on it. Implementing the programme should be entrusted to 'experienced international institutions within the United Nations'. However, there are good reasons to call for the formation of a separate 'World Development Fund', since the additional resources which would be transferred from military expenditure could not be lodged with proven institutions such as the World Bank or the Regional Development Banks, or be at the disposal of the general budget of the United Nations. As everyone knows, not all states belong to the Development Banks – or IMF – and at the United Nations the recipient countries, with their great majority, could make the decisions alone.

Such a proposal takes both the East and the West at their word. Both sides say that disarmament and development belong together, and resources from the first could be used for the other. This verbal unanimity at least offers a chance. And a global initiative in development policy can simultaneously open up a new dimension in global peace policies. Thus, such an initiative should first be prepared in the context of political cooperation between the EEC states, and then discussed with other European partners, as well as with the USA, Canada and Japan. The subject should be introduced into the East–West dialogue in such a way as to give an opportunity of a discussion as unpolemical as possible.

The connection between the necessary long-term change of basic conditions in the world economy, and short-term goals (the special programme) does certainly need further clarification. And overcoming the debt crisis and changing certain IMF practices are not enough. Above all, a joint international effort is called for, and a joint struggle against underdevelopment and negative development, including our own.

VIII

NOT BY BREAD ALONE

In the debate on development policies, economic factors and considerations which do have great weight, are often made to seem absolute. However, we must also keep the historical, cultural and intellectual inheritance of peoples and states and their political opportunities in view. Religious and traditional influences play a part, and so do the legacies of colonial power, and also those models, whether accepted or rejected, which have left their mark on more than one generation of leaders.

Our own experience in Germany of the disastrous consequences of destructive ultra-nationalism should not lead us to close our minds to the new nationalism, often deep-rooted, that we encounter in other parts of the world. Particularly in Africa, boundaries drawn by the colonial powers have divided tribes which share a common culture and language. Islam is gaining ground and making its militant mark on political events, but the fact that Islam is not necessarily militant, and has moderate and non-violent variants, is not widely known. Still less well known is the way in which the cultures of Latin America – the original culture, the culture of the immigrants and later cultural imports – rub against each other and interconnect, whereas over the last few years more attention has been paid to the cultural aspects of social and political change. No one now disputes that school and university education, research and technical training must be taken seriously and encouraged in Third World countries, particularly the least developed of them.

Literacy is of primary importance. UNESCO, the United Nations Educational, Scientific and Cultural Organization, has set itself the objective of eradicating illiteracy by the year 2000, but that is going to take rather longer than envisaged.

- In 1983/4, 29 per cent of the population of the world were unable to read and write.
- In 24 countries, over 70 per cent of adults could not read and write. And despite the great and persistent efforts that are being made, we must expect to see an increase in the *absolute* number of illiterates in the immediate future, owing to rapid population growth.
- In the developing countries, 300 million children between the ages of six and eleven do not go to school at all. And half of those who do go to school leave again before the end of their second year.
- We may expect the number of illiterates to be 900 million at the turn of the century.
- During my Latin American travels in 1984 I myself recorded figures: the illiterates of Brazil, some 30 million of them, were not allowed to take part in the elections; the proportion of illiterates in Peru was estimated to be 18 per cent, although they were not excluded from suffrage there; even in Argentina, there was estimated to be a similar percentage of 'functional' illiterates.
- Can we close our eyes to the depressing fact that, even in 'developed' countries, illiteracy is on the increase again?

Forward-looking North–South policies must give priority to the education of large sections of the population, or it will not be possible for those people to help themselves and further their own interests. However, we should not overestimate the value of formal education. (If that were all that mattered, the Germans would never have let Hitler come to power and wreak such havoc.)

Internationally – assuming that respective conditions are taken into account – we are concerned not just with aid in education and training, but with many additional and as yet unexplored opportunities for scientific, artistic and cultural exchange; not the kind of random exchange whereby skilled personnel are enticed away from developing countries without appropriate recompense. It is also a matter of getting to know the way other people live and think and taking part in something that, despite all public folly, may deserve to be called world culture.

In spite of some justifiable criticism, I think it is deeply to be regretted that UNESCO itself has fallen victim to narrow-mindedness. The USA, having given notice of its impending withdrawal from the organization a year in advance, did in fact withdraw at the beginning of 1985; the large US contribution of 50 million dollars a year is no longer at UNESCO's disposal. The United Kingdom* and some other countries reserved their right to follow the American example.

Washington's attitude is determined by the fact that the present American administration is withdrawing from international organizations where the rules are decided by majorities which cannot very easily be influenced; instead, it is using the more comfortable possibilities of bilateralism. I have already mentioned this in connection with the World Bank's proposals for Africa, the funding of IDA and IFAD, and the International Law of the Sea Convention. America's refusal to accept the jurisdiction of the International Court of Justice in the case of Nicaragua falls into the same category. It should be recalled that some years ago the United States withdrew from the International Labour Organization, which has its headquarters in Geneva, and came back when certain issues had been cleared up.

The decision to withdraw from UNESCO was taken against the advice of various important institutions and people of authority. It was coupled with an assurance that the USA would continue to promote certain UNESCO projects, and would moreover divert the funds saved to other relevant uses.

What, in fact, were the main arguments put forward in the UNESCO dispute?

• It was said that UNESCO had become unacceptably 'politicized', an accusation which makes no sense in those general terms, and whose drift becomes clear only when we know of the imputation that an 'Afro–Arab bloc' has gained excessive influence, with the cooperation of Director General A. M. M'Bow of Senegal – who is to be rated very high as a leading

* Since writing this, the UK has also withdrawn.

figure in the cultural field. (The treatment of Israel as if it were not part of the United Nations lent weight to this allegation.)

- Absurdly, the Director-General and his organization were also supposed to have committed themselves to a new international economic order, though surely anyone must know about the situation at the General Assembly in New York with regard to this matter.

- In my view, the objection that issues of disarmament and peace belong to the controversial field of 'politics', and are thus not within the scope of subjects to be dealt with by the United Nations' cultural organization, is particularly misguided. One might suggest, conversely, that far too little has been done so far to pursue those aspects of the peace issue which are 'not directly political'. If it is true that all wars have begun inside human minds, then human thought and philosophy could surely do a good deal to make lasting peace possible.

- Particular exception was taken to a so-called 'new international communications order', and here pertinent arguments were mixed up with dubious proposals. I would class as dubious those proposals which put the claims of governments before the interests of independent news coverage, while criticism of powerful agencies and media in the North which ignore or take inadequate account of the problems of the South is pertinent. (In my view, independently of criticism from the developing countries, one may object to the fact that the media in our latitudes pay far too little serious attention to Third World issues. News coverage of the United Nations, international organizations and North–South negotiations also leaves much to be desired.)

- There was also criticism of administrative shortcomings and the inflation of the bureaucratic apparatus, something which has become quite usual, not just in international organizations. Among those who raised objections of this nature were many who had thought the political accusations exaggerated, and would have considered it reasonable to concentrate on eliminating shortcomings in administration, routine and excessive expenditure.

The Council of Europe and its advisory assembly have now spoken out clearly in favour of taking seriously the cultural consequences of rapid social and economic change, and acknowledging the great significance to be attached to the cultural dimension in all areas of development cooperation. That includes the duty of protecting a country's artistic heritage and supporting cultural institutes in the developing countries.

Indignation has frequently been expressed in the Third World over the 'organized theft' of works of art, which has its roots in colonialism and thus in history. We are also concerned, however, with the frequent ignoring of the UNESCO convention of 1970, which dealt with measures to forbid and prevent the illicit import, export and acquisition of cultural items, in accordance with which museums and auction rooms should not accept goods illegally offered to them. Critics object to a trade which they rightly consider immoral, and which in fact contributes to annihilating the cultural heritage of the Third World.

Is it asking too much of us to object to such conduct as well? Let us not allow such ideological shadow-fighting as the dispute over UNESCO to obstruct our view!

IX

SEEING IS BETTER THAN HEARING

1. *What Illusions?*

Ever since the early Sixties, the United Nations has repeatedly discussed a proposed fund to be financed from a modest percentage of military expenditure, and to be used for projects to benefit the poor countries. Regular and trivial objections to this proposal have been raised, just as they were raised to the idea of a levy on the arms trade or military spending, as sketched out in the Brandt Report. The present German Minister for Economic Cooperation, Warnke, has contributed an extremely questionable argument to the international debate. One should not, he says, create too close a link between disarmament and development. Connecting these two 'essential and independent aims' over-closely could distract our attention from the need to make progress in each of the two fields. I do not see that treating the two 'essential and independent aims' separately, as hitherto, has been very successful, nor do I see wherein the danger consists of linking them more closely at long last.

The danger lies, rather, in our persistent avoidance of making difficult but necessary decisions. When action is taken against famine and epidemic disease, extortion and its consequences, drug trafficking and criminal syndicates, 'independent' aims are served, but nobody would deny that links exist or dispute their mutual dependence. Certainly no sensible person would insist that measures should be taken to combat theft only if the receiving of stolen goods can be ended at the same time. But neither would anyone wish to separate opposition to one evil from opposition to the other, and claim to be thereby serving the common good.

The economic aspect of an extensive military build-up has not long been the subject of international discussion. But it is being asked, more critically than was previously the case, whether economic order is influenced for the better or destabilized. What will be the effects on the extent, tempo and nature of technical progress? What will be the consequences on infrastructure, education and research relevant to industry in the developing countries? Few would now dispute that armaments and development compete with one another in national budgets.

And many will now also agree that the enormous cost of the arms race does not merely restrict opportunities in development policy, but is a heavy burden on international economic relations. At the same time, we must realize that there is no guarantee that more funds will be available for development if a reduction in military expenditure should be brought about by international agreements. Should such a reduction be made, national needs would be competing with the claims of international aid and cooperation.

Pointing out the negative and harmful effects of the arms race is not enough. We shall have to get rid of the fear that the reconversion from military production to a civil economy will create insoluble problems. More economic cooperation does not necessarily, but *can*, mean more security.

The best historical example of the way in which the transition from war to peace can be made is found in the United States after 1945. The Swedish government has recently made an in-depth study which cogently shows that a change from military to civil production is technically possible and economically advantageous. One might think there were more than enough good arguments for it. But many people, including many of the decision-makers, are not convinced of the need for a basic change in policy until they see that such a change is possible.

Mutual economic dependence can offer hope for world peace. That was how I saw the trade policy components of our own *Ostpolitik*, and that is how I see the diverse forms of cooperation between the various parts of Europe. I am emphatically in agreement with those who regard more intensive interlocking of the world economy as an important factor in a peace policy. But we shall have to guard against the illusion of automatic effects.

There is no room for illusions, not least when they mislead us over deep-seated conflicts of interests and convictions. But do we not find the dangerous illusion-mongers where an outworn realism is cited as an argument for letting the breakneck arms race rush on, while world hunger is ignored? A new kind of realism is called for, one that takes our responsibility for our own heritage and a common future equally seriously.

One can no longer claim with a clear conscience that more armaments automatically mean more security. One can no longer dispute the fact that, on the contrary, humanity is in danger of arming itself to death. Thus, if an end is to be put to this madness in the mutual interest as properly understood, the resources freed must be at least partly made available for productive purposes in the Third World. That may still sound complicated, may seem (may still seem?) beyond our powers of imagination; and we have no familiar criteria.

Compared with the $1,000 billion which it was estimated would be spent on military purposes in 1985, the world makes a ridiculously small contribution to measures for securing peace in the strict sense of the word. If we put the United Nations budget and other international expenditure on peace-keeping measures together, the vast discrepancy is obvious. Globally, three to four hundred times as much is available for military expenditure as for the peaceful resolution of conflicts. It is important for this fact too to be made known to the world, since nothing much changes without the pressure of public opinion. Just 0.1 per cent of worldwide military expenditure would mean trebling the present resources the United Nations has at its disposal for peace-keeping activities.

When the Brandt and Palme Commissions met jointly in Rome in early 1984, we resolved: 'We urgently recommend governments to divert a part of their military expenditure to efforts being made in the fields of development and the securing of peace.' Governments, we said, had been pursuing a policy of confrontation and brought the world to the brink of an economic and military catastrophe. 'The time is ripe for cooperation ... all countries should have the opportunity and obligation to make a contribution to a new system of security ... the United Nations remains the expression of our need for international order.' I would add here that only fitful use has been made of the UN's opportunities of settling conflicts and encouraging the maintenance of peace.

The dream of making the Third World countries into areas free from intervention will find no counterpart in reality. But the idea of removing certain regions and countries from the quarrels of the great powers need not be unrealistic. Internationalizing the 'homemade' conflicts of a region simply involves too many dangers. It ought not to be difficult to make a choice between internationalization of this kind and the neutralizing of a potential source of conflict.

I know that European politics cannot be copied and exported. But among the experiences that most impressed me in the Sixties and early Seventies was the attempt that was made to replace a sterile and dangerous confrontation by limited, realistically significant cooperation, not allowing oneself the illusory belief that ideological opposites can be done away with, but resolving to relieve tensions in a way that might perhaps even help to change the character of the conflict, and could at least decrease its danger. I believe that if we should be spared a major catastrophe it will be possible and worthwhile to build on such experiences. With the help of acceptable intermediate results, practical cooperation and agreements capable of inspiring confidence could improve the political climate, make life easier for humanity, and help to safeguard peace.

It will surprise no one that this view influences my thinking on North–South issues, and I do not see anything wrong with that. I think highly of proceeding step-by-step. It strikes me as more promising than those grand designs which stay put on paper. However, such a strategy can succeed only if we recognize our mutual task and believe in our mutual ability to prevent nuclear war and secure the future of mankind. Any who cherish, even to the slightest degree, yesterday's dream of survival at the expense of others will find the way to fruitful cooperation closed.

One cannot rely on governments to do these things of themselves; most of them need something to set them going.

2. *Polemic Is Not Enough*

Over the last few years, about the most frequently raised objection I have heard is the following: let the East show how *it* is going to give aid first, because the 'aid' it gives, if any, will be only in the form of propaganda and arms. Widespread as this opinion may be in the West, it no longer conforms to the facts.

I write this as one who has long been critical of the foreign policies of the Soviet Union. If I had ever had any illusions, they would have been destroyed by Stalin's power politics and the decisive part they played in the division of Europe. I have observed the marked and frequent way in which Moscow's disarmament initiatives remained mere propaganda. How appallingly unnecessary it has been to make enemies of Czech and Polish reformers; or, within the Soviets' own domain, to treat human rights groups as criminals when they are doing nothing but asserting the principles of the Helsinki declaration of 1975; or to involve themselves in the Afghan venture with its thousands of victims, a venture that will end in neither lasting success nor voluntary approval.

And it is not so long ago that Moscow was clinging to the sterile thesis that the Soviet Union bore no responsibility for the consequences of colonialism, which were to be laid solely at the doors of the Western powers concerned. This was the accepted version, until one day the Third World leaders let it be known they were less interested in the interpretation of past history than in their future; they expected aid from the entire industrialized world, and not just from the Western part of the North. Moreover, it was no secret that countries such as Norway and Sweden made commitments without reference to their noncolonial past, explaining that many problems were not in any case to be ascribed to the colonial past alone.

And here as elsewhere it has turned out that polemic is not enough. If both or all sides had discussed the link between arms and development other than from the propaganda angle, the developing countries and the international community of nations would now be a little further forward. Eastern representatives made the subject a matter of public debate sooner than did others, particularly at the UN, but they did so with an eye firmly fixed on publicity requirements. I think that an effort should long ago have been made, in international forums, to get beyond the clichés which have become so usual there.

Moscow would have made a better showing had it given any prominence to the necessity for development on its home ground, particularly in the Southern and South-Eastern Soviet republics. It could also have been said that aid for allied countries figured larger than indicated in the statistics of the OECD or the World Bank. In 1980, the development committee of the OECD made an interesting emendation. Between one year and another, the estimated proportion of the Soviet gross national product devoted to development aid went up from 0.03 to 0.14 per cent. The explanation of this remarkable swing lies in the question of whether Cuba, Vietnam and North Korea are included or not. (The unfortunate habit of adding up military and economic aid, and thus confusing them, is not confined to the Soviet Union, but is embodied in the budgetary laws of the USA as well.)

That example shows that polemic is no substitute for checking figures. There has been some movement on the Eastern side; positions ranging from the dubious to the untenable have been examined. Scientists, quite rightly, have been somewhat ahead of the members of the political machine. Politicians active in the fields of economics and particularly of trade were ahead of those civil servants whose concern was the inheritance of the Communist International.

The tendency of world powers to meddle in the affairs of other countries has given rise to unprofitable polemic as well. What are the differences in the form this tendency takes? What is the specific relationship between power politics and ideology? We may doubt whether the race for the Third World and the absurdly excessive arms build-up can be moderated and controlled. But surely we must keep on trying if there is still, or again, to be any idea, for more than a brief moment, of reducing dangerous tensions?

It was no accident that the superpowers resumed their exchange of information about certain critical regions when they had agreed to new negotiations over the arms race and its possible limitation. One thinks first of the Middle East and Central America, but South-East Asia and southern Africa are in an

equally critical state. And many people are unaware how dangerous the conflict over the Islas Malvinas (Falkland Islands) could
have been if their 'nuclearization' had brought countermeasures
in its wake, if only on the nature of plans, at first.

Reinforcement of the peace-keeping functions of the United
Nations is essential for a policy of peace. These functions come
within the scope of the Secretary General and in particular of the
Security Council; the opportunities both offer for the settlement
of differences should be extended and used more freely.

In the second half of the Seventies, the two superpowers tried to
come to an agreement on the limitation of arms exports. Both
sides thought at the time that this was more sensible than simply
calling each other names. It does not look as if further progress
will be easy. But the future belongs to those who are capable of
applying themselves afresh to the problems of East–West and
North–South relations, armaments and the economy.

A special conference of the United Nations is planned for the
summer of 1986, on the subject of 'Disarmament and Development'. The French government has been particularly strong in its
advocacy of this conference. A few years ago, a group of experts
chaired by Inga Thorsson of Sweden did preliminary work for the
UN Secretary-General. Important initiatives have also come from
the Disarmament Committee of the Socialist International,
chaired by Kalevi Sorsa, Prime Minister of Finland.

In April 1985, prominent representatives of East and West,
North and South met at the headquarters of the United Nations.
'Survival in the nuclear age' was the subject of the symposium
which I was asked to chair. We stated that:

There is a dynamic triangular relationship between disarmament, development and security. As long as the arms race
continues, particularly where nuclear weapons are concerned,
the world will not succeed in achieving either more stable and
harmonious social and economic development within a more
lasting international economic and political order, or global
and national security. Competition in the field of armaments –
quantitative and qualitative, conventional and nuclear – has
had extremely harmful economic and social effects on the
people of all nations, both rich and poor. If even a fraction of

the valuable resources now being swallowed up by excessive military expenditure were diverted to social and economic development, particularly to combating the poverty of two-thirds of the world's population, it would make a very considerable improvement to life and security on our planet.

That New York statement continued:

This enormous and increasing amount of military expenditure is economically harmful, giving rise to inequity and distortion, and has contributed to the present deterioration of the international economic situation. Moreover, the spread of militaristic culture to the developing countries does further harm. The consequence of failure to control the arms race has been more confrontation and distrust, and the priority given to security issues has had unfortunate results not just for détente between East and West, but also for North–South cooperation.

We suggested that: 'Governments should plan and prepare for a process of the transfer of resources from military to civil uses. This would also, and not least, increase confidence in their serious wish for genuine disarmament.'

3. Changes in the East

Not surprisingly, I have been repeatedly asked since the formation of my Commission in 1977 why I invited no members from the Soviet Union, the Warsaw Pact states and the People's Republic of China to sit on it. The idea did arise, and I was certainly not hostile to it. However, I did not then think the time had come. Later, I was surprised to find that some people were absolutely set against having Russian representation on the Commission, and yet gave the opposite impression in public.

Our colleagues *did* manage to make contacts at the time, visiting Moscow and Peking on behalf of the Commission. I was able to form my own opinion in conversation with prominent people in the Eastern European states. In the summer of 1977,

Brezhnev said in a letter, 'that we approach the problem of relations between former colonial countries in a rather different way from the representatives of the Western states'. However, he said, they were ready to discuss contacts with the Commission.

Interest, mild at first and then greater, was shown in other quarters too. As one of the more open-minded of Eastern statesmen said: 'We cannot be indifferent to matters concerning future conditions of world trade, or the elements of a new international monetary system, or the international aspects of energy and food supplies.' That is as true as ever; some new problems have arisen since that statement was made, some have become more acute over the years. But while more contacts and talks would have been needed at least for discussion of certain practical and fundamental questions, and an agreement on them if possible, the gulf between the superpowers and the power blocs has grown even wider. Such a state of affairs need not persist. If détente were to figure more prominently on the international agenda again, North–South policies would benefit as well.

In Moscow, as elsewhere, I was able to discuss North–South issues as not just a human and political challenge, but a dangerous time-bomb. There was and there is a good reason to speak out *everywhere*, as distinctly as need be, on the disproportion between world armament and world development. It was therefore important that Soviet reaction to my Commission's second report was receptive on this point. The Soviet leadership wrote to me: 'Your report correctly indicates a direct connection between disarmament and the world's socio-economic progress.' The task ahead, said this letter, lay in actually putting an end to the arms race and employing the resources thus saved to solve the most pressing problems 'which a considerable part of humanity faces: hunger, disease and illiteracy'.

A leading Polish economist pointed out that there have been considerable changes in the policy of Comecon: until the end of the Sixties, the belief that the Soviet/Socialist economic model could be exported to the developing countries prevailed. Since then, he says, the basic premise has been that the right preconditions must be created in the countries concerned before 'a Socialist concept suited to varying conditions' could be introduced. It was also acknowledged that until the end of the Seventies, the former colonial powers were held to blame for the backwardness of the Third World; there was a widespread view that the Socialist states were not responsible for the misery in the poor and the poorest countries.

When I talked to Leonid Brezhnev in the Kremlin at the beginning of July 1981, he raised the subject of his own accord; he knew I would be mentioning it anyway, and was more forthcoming than before. He did not, he said, rule out the possibility of the Soviet Union's taking part in the planned summit meeting at Cancun: 'We do not say it will not be possible for us to participate in some way.' Some of the old arguments came up again: Moscow bore no real responsibility, and why did Western commentators rely on false statistics? We based our claims, he said, on figures which did not correspond to the facts. Why did we not count Soviet aid to Cuba and Vietnam, which were surely developing countries?

During my visit to Moscow in 1981, I went to the Institute of International Economics of the Academy of Sciences, of which the late Professor Inosemzev was principal at the time, and was impressed by the intellectual vigour more prevalent here than where politics alone were discussed. I spoke to a sizeable audience of professors and lecturers on 'issues which transcend political systems'. Despite our differing ritual in the way of presentation and expression, we soon found ourselves on the same wavelength. The scientists there knew what was in store for humanity, quite apart from political orders and social systems.

I had an opportunity to elaborate on this at the end of 1981, in Budapest, when representatives of institutes for development research from both sides of Europe invited me to a joint conference. The relationship between East and West, I said, still a tense one, and intolerably burdened by the arms race, and the extremely unsatisfactory relationship between North and South, were interconnected in a complicated and unhealthy manner. The industrial states of the North – in the East as in the West – were not, I continued, in a position to halt the squandering of the earth's natural resources and the laying waste of our planet in both North and South: 'Nor are they in a position to enable the developing countries to prosper, although that would promote their own economic wellbeing. This is a situation which will appear utterly absurd to future historians, should there be any; they will find it impossible to understand our present world's incapacity for action.'

Moreover, I said, the way in which interconnected problems were separated as if they had nothing to do with each other prevented this state of affairs from being rectified: 'That is the case with East–West and North–South relations and with interdependence between the two planes. It is the case with economic, ecological and militaristic issues. We must tackle these problems today in awareness of our mutual dependence, and in whatever area we are concerned, we must do so not in competition with each other, but jointly. Global and common or complementary solutions call for global negotiations.'

The great powers must thus include the dimension of North–South relations and of the global problems I have described in their policies, or they ensure their failure as we enter upon a new millennium. Creating concrete links, at long last, between the East–West issue and the North–South issue, bringing together détente and disarmament on the one hand and developmental and environmental policies on the other – for this there is no reasonable way without including the Comecon states in discussion of these questions. The Soviet Union is well known to have developed into a self-sufficient economic system, helped by the fact that it depends upon hardly any imported commodities. It has also long practised political exclusivity, so that no closer network of economic relations could be formed. Time has passed that attitude by. In future, if states allied to the Soviet Union want to reach their specific goals, they will have to depend more than hitherto on the exchange of goods with the rest of the world, and will be increasingly called upon to face problems of a global character, particularly in international environmental, energy and food programmes. The Soviet Union is in a rather unenviable situation, since its own agricultural performance has time and again fallen far short of the targets it has set itself.

Early in 1985, a study from the Friedrich-Ebert Foundation of economic cooperation in Third World countries said: 'The Soviet Union, which until quite recently rejected the idea of East–West cooperation in Third World countries on ideological grounds, is today regarded as the driving force and principal instigator of such kinds of cooperative action.' At the end of the Sixties, only Romania and non-aligned Yugoslavia showed not just readiness in principle but a lively interest in cooperating with Western partners in third countries. Of recent years, however, the Comecon states have succeeded, says this study, 'in securing considerable shares of the market in developing countries which used to be exclusively the province of Western industrial states'.

The East shows willingness, though one may not sense such receptivity to North–South issues everywhere as that of Janos Kadar, the Hungarian leader. Setting out from the appreciably different conditions of his own country, Todor Zhivkov assured me at the end of 1984 that he wanted to increase Bulgaria's small amount of trade with the Third World. And even Bulgaria has over 10,000 experts participating in projects in various countries anyway.

The German Democratic Republic is pursuing an active (also an ideologically active) policy in a number of Third World countries. In the economic area it has embarked upon joint projects with firms from the Federal Republic of Germany, in Libya and Ethiopia, for instance. What better could we wish for than more consistent joint action for the good of the developing countries on the part of the two German states, extending beyond isolated cases of cooperation?

Over the last few years, the People's Republic of Poland has been impeded in its economic as well as political activities abroad by its difficulties at home. But one success to Warsaw's name was the fact that in early 1985, there were no more apparent misgivings, even in the USA, about its application for membership of the International Monetary Fund. Romania and Hungary had been able to take that step some years earlier. Czechoslovakia, like the German Democratic Republic and Bulgaria, registered a distinct increase in business with the Third World.

The Comecon states are obviously trying to remove their ideological blinkers where the developing countries and international economic cooperation are concerned. Of course there is an understandable element of self-interest involved. Cooperation extends their own freedom of movement. Resolution of the principal differences between the Eastern and Western systems is not within the realm of possibility, but cooperation to the mutual advantage of both sides is, and so are measures to secure peace, and the definition of system-bridging interests. That seems to be the motto of the new Soviet General-Secretary. When I talked to Mikhail Gorbachev at the end of May 1985, I found increased interest, which I had not really expected, in two areas: North–South relations and Europe. An Eastern aphorism is thus confirmed: to see something once is better than to hear about it a hundred times.

4. *Peking and Delhi*

In the spring of 1984, I was asked by a newspaper what human achievement most impressed me. My answer was: 'The fact, if it is a fact, that China can feed a billion people.' After my visit to China in the early summer of 1984, which I had had to postpone several times, I would no longer have made that reservation 'if it is a fact'. Indeed, astonishing as it might sound, there was even talk of a certain grain *surplus* at the beginning of 1985.

Naturally one must not overestimate one's own impressions on a foreign tour. But I checked with well-informed foreign observers, and they confirmed the fact that since 1964, no Chinese had died of starvation. I consider this sober observation one of the great positive experiences of my time.

It is not for me to assess the economic reforms which the People's Republic of China – largely self-sufficient, and comparable to the Soviet Union only in that – has recently decided to push through. The combination of intensive agriculture, with clear incentives for farmers, and the production of consumer goods leaped to my eye and carried conviction. In Peking and Canton, and most of all in Shanghai, I saw busy urban life and considerable economic activity, and also real instances of European and Chinese industrial cooperation; there are good opportunities open to our own firms if they make the appropriate effort.

The industrial production of a city like Shanghai is, in absolute figures, four times that of Hong Kong and ten times that of Singapore. The thirst for knowledge and multiplicity of cultural activities exceed anything we in Europe can imagine of China.

Incidentally, when I was speaking on North–South issues at a Shanghai university, I was asked to use my own mother tongue; they needed no translation from the German! (The university was founded by Germans before the First World War, and continued its association with Germany – both West and East – after 1945.) The pressure of population is reflected in the severe lack of living space: 3.5 square metres per head in Shanghai. In the city itself, 6.7 million people live on a third of the surface area of Hamburg (with just over one million inhabitants).

During my talks in Peking I was able to take as a starting point the fact that China had already engaged in the difficult North–South dialogue. It had taken its place in IMF and the World Bank, without yet being conspicuous there for its contributions to the proceedings. It had also turned its attention to the Group of 77, and taken an interest in the efforts at South–South cooperation being made. I was aware that the People's Republic had varying experience of aid projects in some of the poorest countries, but I did not know that wind-powered pumps and the use of biogas to generate energy were now playing a considerable part in China itself.

The now legendary Deng Xiaoping was not lacking in self-confidence: international politics, he said, was not a card game in which China could be used as one of the cards. General-Secretary Hu Yaobang spoke of his people's wish to work with the people of Europe and the whole world for détente and an end to the arms race, adding that the emergence of the Third World into the international arena was an extremely important phenomenon of our time and also a powerful factor for the maintenance of world peace. 'China belongs to the Third World, and for better or worse is linked with Third World countries. China considers the preservation of the rights and interests of the countries of the Third World its international duty; it resolutely supports the Third World in its struggle for national independence and sovereignty, for the development of its countries' respective national economies, and for the creation of a new international economic order.'

Hu was in favour of support for the North–South dialogue, and declared his intention of taking an active part in South–South cooperation. The industrial countries, he said, should respect the independence and sovereignty of the countries of the Third

World, and pursue economic and trade policies advantageous to those countries. He thought that 'far-sighted leading figures in the developed countries' had seen that such a policy towards Third World countries would also benefit themselves in the long run. The Chinese party leader identified himself with my tenet that peace must come before ideology. He approved of my and my friends' ideas on the connection between disarmament and development.

I took with me to Delhi a critical remark to the effect that India might do well to restrain its 'sub-hegemonistic tendencies'. In answer to that, Indira Gandhi wondered ironically what plans the Chinese had for their own periphery. To counterbalance the ASEAN group mentioned earlier, India is in the process of preparing for a regional collaboration in South Asia, in which Bangladesh, Bhutan, the Maldives, Nepal, Pakistan and Sri Lanka are to participate. Agriculture, rural development, health and population issues are on the agenda for the envisaged exchange of opinions.

My visits to these two very large Asian countries gave rise to some comparative considerations, particularly with regard to population growth and food production.

The Chinese figures are well known. China's population of 542 million inhabitants at the time of the 1949 revolution had almost doubled to one billion by 1980. Since then there has been further growth. Officially, the population is to be kept below 1.2 billion and will stabilize after the year 2000. So far as total population is concerned, India will catch up with the Chinese. At the time of Independence in 1947, it had about 350 million inhabitants. In 1984, that figure had grown to 730 million, it will be a billion at the turn of the century, and is not expected to stabilize until the year 2060.

High priority has been given to birth control in both countries ever since the early Seventies, under state auspices. But there have been and still are great problems. Not all Chinese observe the norm of a single-child family, and many fail to observe it in spite of serious material disadvantages. And again and again one hears reports of parents wanting their only child to be a son. In one outlying province, there were recently found to be three times as many boys as girls among children under three . . . In India, Prime

Minister Nehru introduced a family planning programme at the end of the Fifties, with moderate success. Two decades later, under his daughter Indira Gandhi, an attempt to conduct a programme of compulsory mass sterilization failed.

The success of the Chinese in increasing food production to the point where hunger was overcome has won worldwide notice and respect. Comparatively speaking, less notice has been taken of the fact that India too can now supply its own needs. Grain production has quadrupled since 1967, and recently some rice has even been exported. Food production and population growth have almost reached equilibrium. A great achievement, in large part due to producers' cooperatives. However, almost half the entire population still lives below the poverty line. The lack of public health care is still alarming, although great efforts have been undertaken in this field too. Almost half the population still cannot read and write. It has been shown that farmers produce more not just when modern technology and modern means of marketing are available, but when enough serious attention is paid to the requirements of public education and health care.

India has made considerable progress along the road to becoming a great economic nation. It now has a large industrial sector, a highly developed technology, and a large number of skilled workers. A better balanced development of agriculture and industry could have beneficial consequences as a whole. One should learn from one's neighbours. North Korean agriculture is well spoken of. In some Asian countries which, like Taiwan, have intensively speeded up industrialization, agriculture does not seem to have kept pace.

5. Wasted Chances in Central America

On 25 October 1984, the Contadora document was to have been signed. That event did not take place; the United States thought it would not be in its own interests to sign, and won first Honduras and then other Central American governments over to its side.

Contadora is the name of an island where the conditions of a peace treaty for Central America were first discussed and then negotiated. The participants represented the Presidents of Colombia, Mexico, Panama and Venezuela. President Betancur of Colombia, whom I met at the time when the project failed, said it was as if the creation of the world had been interrupted on the fourth day, adding that every day that passed without major warfare meant success for Contadora. Who would have wished to dispute that? And who would not have been glad to hear that the heads of state concerned intended to continue their efforts, as all four of them told me?

In those October weeks Nicaragua was preparing for the elections to be held in early November, in which part of the opposition refused to take part; their American 'advisers' were against participation in the elections, just as they were against a ceasefire in the north of Nicaragua at the Honduran border; they flatly declined to exert a moderating influence on the Contras, the sworn enemies of the Sandinistas who have held power since the revolution. Instead, the unofficial war went on, in intensified form – involving intervention, sabotage, and economic strangulation. As a result, the Sandinistas became more dependent than would otherwise have been expected, and more than most of them liked, upon help from the Eastern bloc. There is no doubt the Soviet leadership would not miss any opportunity to needle its rival superpower.

It was nevertheless misleading to press the focal point of Central American crisis into the pattern of the East–West conflict. Even Henry Kissinger, despite his usually conservative position, held economic and social circumstances chiefly to blame for the crisis in that region. His Commission called for an aid programme, setting its immediate financial requirements at $1 billion.

The USA have always considered Central America and the Caribbean their back yard and the province of their big business. Their monopolistic claim to intervention in the area leaned heavily on indigenous oligarchies and 'friendly' governments, even when those governments might be brutally abusing power and opposing all the demands of democratic and social renewal. There have been other cases of the United States repeatedly allowing chances in the Third World to slip away, on narrow economic grounds and for reasons of ideological prejudice – the

East–West angle, lack of understanding for liberation movements.

As time went by, Central America increasingly became an arena for terror and persecution, a *danse macabre* of violence and counter-violence:

- Daniel Oduber, the former President of Costa Rica, estimates that there have been 150,000 to 200,000 victims of violence there since 1978.
- In Nicaragua, Somoza's reign of terror, the counter-violence it provoked, and the ensuing conflicts left some 60,000 dead. The estimate for 1978–79 alone is 35,000 dead, 100,000 wounded, and 40,000 children orphaned – and that with a population of less than three million. In 1984 the Contras were responsible for 5,000 victims.
- In El Salvador, between 20,000 and 40,000 civilians have so far fallen victim to oppression and civil strife.
- Guatemala has been the scene of particularly inhuman action against the Indians. Since the military seized power, 35,000 people have 'disappeared'. In the spring of 1985, colleagues of mine in the German Parliament, the Bundestag, who were touring the country ascertained that families are threatened if they search for disappeared relatives.
- Honduras, with its repeated violations of human rights, is not known to be governed according to the principles of a Quaker community either; recently there have been reports that leading military men are inclined towards taking an independent course.
- Here we should also remember the balance sheet of terror in the *South* American military dictatorships; 15,000 dead in Chile, 9,000 'disappeared' in Argentina, and many other deaths as well.

When Gabriel García Marquez received his Nobel Prize in Stockholm in 1982, he said: 'The country which could be formed of all who have been forcibly exiled and made to emigrate from Latin America would have a larger population than Norway.'

I would not want to pretend that I have been convinced by all

the measures and views of Nicaragua's revolutionary government. But I have been able to assure myself of its determination to
carry out reforms in the framework of a mixed economy system.
And despite all untoward events, it has also achieved some
notable successes, particularly in the struggle against illiteracy.
The leadership was prepared to undertake a series of measures to
work for the recovery of the country's economy. However, the
opposition of Washington stood in the way of a loan from the
Inter-American Development Bank.

The government in Managua was ready to sign the Contadora
agreement, to pledge itself to non-intervention, and to guarantee
that foreign military advisers should withdraw and no foreign
bases be established. In Havana, Fidel Castro assured me that he
too would accept corresponding obligations. In any case, conditions in Central America in his view are not such that the Cuban
model could be exported there. No doubt analysis of Cuba's own
interests lay behind that statement.

To return to October 1984: in La Palma, the parties to the
Salvadorean civil war faced each other in talks for the first time.
The Christian Democrat President, Napoleon Duarte, regarded
with distrust by the extreme right, met representatives of the
political and military opposition; since then there have been a few
limited ceasefire periods. There is the suggestion of a chance for a
peaceful solution. However, if Nicaragua were to suffer actual
invasion, or were forced to its knees by some other means, there
would be an intensification of guerrilla warfare in El Salvador,
and it would flare up again in large parts of the region.

In that same autumn of 1984 the Foreign Ministers of the
countries of the European Community, together with those of
Spain and Portugal, met their counterparts of the Central American states and the Contadora group in San José, the capital of
Costa Rica. The actual substance of the meeting was slight, but it
had symbolic significance. It was not that anyone had forgotten
what the map looks like, or would have wished to offend the USA.
The idea was to demonstrate European interests, the wish for
cooperation and at the same time the readiness to support those
forces working for peace. I do not overrate the possibilities. But
there is now a persistent demand in Central and South America
for more cooperation with Europe. When the Commission of the

European Community announced a skeleton agreement for co-operation with Latin America at the end of 1984, the response was greater than actually justified by the content of the agreement.

What about Fidel Castro? He has shown how dubious a proceeding it is to try to master a national and social revolutionary movement by means of isolation and intervention. Castro has developed statesmanlike qualities, though Cuban military commitments may seem to suggest the opposite. His caution in Central American affairs is unmistakable; so is his wish for relations with the USA. Castro, who had tried to steer the non-aligned countries towards Moscow, now realizes how diverse the Third World is and in what a variety of ways it manifests itself.

He considers important what developing countries can do for each other, not least in the areas of health and education. Here we may sense a certain pride in the fact that Cuba and Costa Rica have achieved more than any other Latin American countries to provide schools and hospitals, 'leaving behind some industrial countries'; they even send doctors abroad, and there is thus no lack of reference to the fact that doctors sent from Western countries to the Third World cost very much more than Cuban doctors, for Cuba requires no direct payment in return.

Not everything one hears about Cuban agriculture is on the positive side. But if you fly over the island you cannot but be impressed by the progress being made in afforestation. Little has as yet been written about the role of deforestation in the Central American and Caribbean countries in causing their wretched living conditions. El Salvador is not the only place where the deforestation of a country has contributed to a crisis. More than any other part of the Caribbean, Haiti, a country known in literature as a 'land of woods and waters', now has more up-rooted people than other parts of the Caribbean, people driven from the countryside by environmental causes, and Jamaica is a similar case.

6. *The Middle East*

The conflict between the superpowers has had particularly grave effects in the Middle East. The clash of their interests has mingled with the inter-Arab dispute and the antagonism between Arabs and Israelis. In recent years, two-thirds of worldwide arms supplies to the developing countries have gone to countries of the Near and Middle East.

- The United States indirectly became the protector of Saudi Arabia and the smaller, conservative oil states; up to 1978 the USA had close economic and military connections with the Shah of Iran; most important of all, it has guaranteed the existence of Israel, a country which is, of course, well able to assert itself too.
- The Soviet Union formed close links with Syria, and found Libya a solvent customer for armaments. Under President Nasser, it won influence in Egypt which then passed largely to the Americans under Sadat.
- The war between Iraq and Iran – both of them non-aligned countries – which has now dragged on for over half a decade is largely waged with imported weapons; before it began the Soviet Union had equipped one state and the USA the other.
- If it had been possible to impose an effective arms embargo on Iran and Iraq, that war would have been over long ago. Cynics add that weapons can be tested only on the battlefields of war. Saudi Arabia and the Gulf states spend 40 billion dollars a year on defence, by now rather because they fear Iran than out of any desire to attack Israel.
- Jordan is trying to obtain authority to negotiate for the Palestinians in its forthcoming negotiations with Israel. At the same time, it is anxious not to be entirely dependent on the West, but to have access to Soviet backing (and weapons).

The above summary indicates only a few of the threads that go to make up the Middle Eastern tangle. Who would venture to predict when it will be unravelled, or whether partial agreements between Israel and its immediate neighbours will last? Both superpowers have an obvious interest in limiting these conflicts and not leaving their respective allies and protégés to themselves. Hence there were confidential contacts over the Gulf War, and they agreed, early in 1985, not indeed to aim for an international conference on the Middle East, but to have an exchange of opinions without any commitments. Arms deliveries across frontiers are the order of the day in the Gulf War. A German firm – a large share held by Iran – delivered troop carriers to Iraq through its Brazilian subsidiary. Another firm on friendly terms with the first sent Iran tanks by way of its Argentinian partner. Italy has sent helicopters to one side and frigates to the other. Germany and other members of the European Community have exported electronic equipment to both sides at once. I will not go on with the list, but state my firm belief that the Federal Republic of Germany would be well advised to keep out of the international arms trade, particularly in the Middle East, even when others would then deliver the supplies.

When I was in Israel at the end of January, 1985, much of my time was occupied in talking to Arabs with responsibilities in that country itself, on the West Bank and in Gaza. My abiding impression was that small steps in the humanitarian, administrative and economic fields could serve as confidence-building measures on the way to a peaceful order. Israel had then begun withdrawing troops from the Lebanon. It urged the Egyptians to activate diplomatic relations. Jordan was informed what obvious subjects could be important in negotiations.

Prospects had once looked much worse. In this part of the world, as elsewhere, chances have been missed and wasted – by all concerned. But one chance has lain unused, never yet brought seriously into play. It revealed itself to me for the first time when, in the summer of 1978, with Kreisky in Vienna, I was present at a meeting between Anwar Sadat and Shimon Peres. Once matters of protocol and the politics of the day had been dealt with, both leaders turned to look at the future. A fascinating prospect opened – what could not be achieved if willingness to cooperate replaced military categories and destructive capacity! I could not but think of this memorable meeting when our Commission and other committees had to deal with the increasing militarization of the Third World.

The two participants in those talks at Vienna soon turned their attention to detailed discussion of ways whereby deserts might be made into fertile land, backward areas filled with productive activity, and to possible ways of promoting industry and the practical application of modern technological experience. It was an encouraging indication that solutions other than military ones can be found, even in the conflicts of the Middle East. Indeed, that in the last resort there can *only* be other solutions.

And deliberations such as those I have mentioned are not over. A promising attempt is being made to concentrate on the economic development of the entire region. We need not call on the Marshall Plan as a model in any narrow sense, and its scheme could not be transferred to that area. But I would like to plead for the superpowers, the Europeans, the Arab world and the Israelis to make an effort to clear the rubble away *together*, and to promote and stabilize the economic development of the region.

Nothing, of course, gets over the fact that the Palestinian question has come to occupy the centre of the Arab–Israeli conflict. That was how my friend Nahum Goldmann, for many years President of the World Jewish Congress, saw it himself. However, the important point should be to go on from stabilization of the dangerously volatile situation to genuine cooperation. And one must hope that it will then be possible to make progress in the struggle against the dangers of mutual destruction.

The Arab world, like Israel, has highly gifted people and great leaders. There can be no doubt that great progress is also being made there in the fields of science and technology, trade and industry. Model social institutions are coming into existence in many places; such is the case with oil-rich Kuwait. It is also true that relatively speaking, the oil states have done more than the industrial states for the developing countries. (Which does not, however, alter the fact that great poverty is to be found in the Arab world itself as far as the North African Maghreb region.)

I repeat: the question is whether, and when, use will be made in the Middle East of the chance which resides in sharing Israel's highly developed scientific and practical skills, not least in the field of agriculture. Israel is ahead of many other countries; its practical knowledge could be turned to good account not just for its neighbours but for the Third World in general. (It should be added that I speak not *only* of future prospects, for Israel is already successfully cooperating with several countries in Latin America and Africa.)

Anyone wishing to see what can be done with difficult soil should go and see what has been done on the spot. That may be said of more than one country. At the end of 1984, for instance, I saw for myself at the excellent Institute of Agrarian Science outside Sofia what has been done there to improve poor soil, to desalinate other types of soil, and to make soil destroyed by industry fertile again. This is a subject upon which work is being done in the Middle East, as it is in other parts of the Third World. The experience of Pakistan is regarded as so encouraging that it could be used in the Sahel zone.

Water is so important to this region that a member of the Egyptian government recently said he thought the next war could break out over it – the Nile, he meant, not politics. So far as irrigation is concerned, the Israelis, not the Kuwaitis, are ahead of many others:

- They have long been able to desalinate sea water, but this is a costly process, because of the high amount of energy consumed, and will have to wait some time longer.
- Besides making extremely good use of what water is present, the Israelis have been using brackish water in the cultivation of vegetable crops for a number of years.
- Over the last few years, they have succeeded in using sea water to irrigate several varieties of vegetable and grain crops. The process involves a drip system and plastic containers to filter out the salt and keep it from damaging the soil. Complicated, certainly, but think of the possibilities!

My Arab friends have not always understood why I would not associate myself with demands for normalization of the Middle East situation which neglected historical experience. However, I am the citizen of a country which will long have to bear the burden of its own history, and must never forget the responsibility laid upon it. What might appear normal could in the last resort be well-concealed brutality.

Facts are facts, and no one must be allowed to distort them. And there is no other way in which cooperation with the Arabs could really succeed; one cannot cheat by disregarding vital elements in the lives of nations.

7. *Development Aid for War*

International arms trade is a profitable business. Just how profitable one would not only gather from the Brandt report. Suppliers both old and new have between them distributed a scarcely imaginable potential for destruction all over the globe, and they even advertise the fact as well. Is it not, we asked, macabre to see so rapid and dynamic a transfer of ultra-modern technology from rich to poor countries in the area of deadly weaponry? As Alva Myrdal said: 'More and more states are buying more and more insecurity at a higher and higher price.'

The militarization of the Third World increases the incalculable risks for the superpowers as well. Their attempt to come to an agreement on the limitation of arms exports was broken off even before a new administration came to power in Washington. It is now more than uncertain whether the subject will arise again should the powers make any progress over the limitation of nuclear weapons.

In 1983 the Stockholm International Peace Research Institute (SIPRI) made the interesting and at first glance encouraging observation that world trade in conventional weapons was slightly on the decline. The reason was seen in the scarcity of money of the Third World. However, presumably an increase in the domestic production of arms has begun to play a part. And the situation as a whole was still far from inspiring optimism:

- In 1983, the monetary value of the arms *trade* was set at $135 billion, 70 per cent of that amount being the share of the two superpowers.
- The two superpowers were responsible for half of worldwide expenditure on *armaments*, and all industrial countries together for two-thirds. The share of the developing countries, including the oil states but not China, was some 20 per cent; twenty years ago it was all of 6 per cent!

- The two superpowers incontestably head the lists of big arms dealers, with a growing tendency for the USA to take the lead.

The American list of customers is twice as long as the Russian list: 39 major buyers as against 16, and in addition the USA are more generous in allocating production licences to Third World countries. Next on the list of arms suppliers come the West Europeans, first France, then the United Kingdom, the Federal Republic of Germany (with an increasing share) and Italy. The list continues with Czechoslovakia, Poland, North Korea, Brazil, Spain, South Korea, Israel and Switzerland. Recently China, South Africa, India and Egypt have featured on it too. In 1984 Brazil's dynamic arms industry made great strides in competition with the world's other arms exporters; its volume of exports reached some three billion dollars. An arms deal to the value of $1 billion was concluded with Saudi Arabia at the end of 1984.

As regards arms *importers*, SIPRI and the American Arms Control Agency are agreed, though they are not quite unanimous over exact ranking, that the leading group consists of Syria, Libya, Saudi Arabia, Iran, Iraq, Egypt and Algeria. India and Indonesia also figure prominently. By now a quarter of the accumulated debts of the Third World are due to arms imports; the financial difficulties of the countries affected exercise a slightly moderating influence on arms buying. In some of the Latin American countries there is debate as to whether the new democracies must accept responsibility for everything the military dictators imported, making the burden of debt even heavier.

There is no doubt that the extent and nature of a country's military equipment has become a kind of status symbol in many parts of the Third World. In military dictatorships in particular, arms are a regular fetish. At the same time – and why hide it? – a country's military organization has sometimes had beneficial effects on literacy, road-building and other forms of modest modernization.

In Washington, Congress's research service calculated that the United States encourages bankrupt states to buy weapons which they often do not need, paying with money they do not have. Mark Hatfield, the Republican Senator from Oregon who is committed to a peace policy and who presented this study, called the present policy 'short-sighted'; he will have realized that that would be regarded as understatement. To give an illustration: in 1982–84, American aid for Africa rose by 40 per cent, but sales and donations of arms, by 150 per cent.

The rapid build-up of armaments industries in parts of the Third World has resulted in drastic changes on the international arms markets. Some countries are increasingly in competition in third country markets with the traditionally dominant arms industries, and are themselves now exporting to the industrial countries. As I have mentioned, Brazil is one of the biggest arms manufacturers in the world. There as elsewhere, they are trying to boost exports so as to lower unit costs and improve the balance of goods and services. Argentina feels positively dependent on the export of armaments. (Iran is not the only place where those tanks built with German assistance end up.)

About 40 developing countries now have their own industries manufacturing tanks, artillery and aeroplanes. The tendency is to move from production under licence to development on their own account. It is not so long since the developing countries had only a 5 per cent share in global expenditure on military research and development, while the share of the two superpowers was 80 per cent.

The Palme Report observed, much to the point: 'The major proportion of military budgets may be allocated to the payment of soldiers and civilian employees, and governments also obtain goods, services and buildings for defence purposes from the civil area. But since the beginning of the Eighties, expenditure on special military equipment and defence research has shown the biggest rise.' And further: 'More and more developing countries are importing technically sophisticated weapons systems, which must often be financed as normal purchases and not with military aid.'

The obsession with troops and weapons of many who bear responsibility in the Third World – laudable exceptions only confirm the rule – is unforgivable and cannot, objectively speaking, be excused. I say so at every opportunity, including in personal conversations. However, it is too easy to condemn the arms importers alone, and not address oneself at least as forcibly to those governments which supply or at least sanction the supply of arms.

What is more, it would be easy to prevent importing countries from spending development aid funds on armaments. One knows, after all, to whom money should be paid. It is quite another matter to know whether development aid is freeing a country's own resources for armaments purposes. However, the following forms part of an unvarnished picture of reality: food production decreased in the African countries south of the Sahara during the Seventies, and thus before the latest drought disaster, while in view of population growth it ought to have increased. Arms supplies to that region tended to rise; but funds were not available for fertilizers and pesticides.

Today no one speaks out openly in opposition when concern for security is associated with the economic objections to arms exports – war development aid! The militarization of the Third World increases the already considerable risks to world peace.

The proposal to set up a register of arms exports at the United Nations, which would also register plants destined for arms manufacture, deserves support, even if it does not attack the root cause of the problem. But one must not aim too high, and in view of the enormous increases of the past few years, registering and thus partially controlling arms production and export would represent some progress.

8. *A Just War?*

We know the saying that war is the continuation of politics by other means: once a viable calculation, as the question of which side represented historical progress was once viable. In the conditions of the imperialistic world system, *prevention* of war was at the heart of progressive foreign policy for large minorities. That did not alter the fact that in the face of Hitler's murderous régime, the embodiment of imperialism of a newly dangerous nature, the clear victory of one side over the other was necessarily desirable.

Among the most important outcomes of the Second World War besides the breaking of Fascism as a national power, were the rise of the USA and the Soviet Union to the status of world powers, the ending of old-style colonialism – not exactly as some had expected; and – most important – the qualitative stride forward in arms development: the first manufacture and the first use of atomic bombs. After that, and not before, nothing was the same as it had been, unwilling as many still are to accept realization of that qualitative change, or readily as they have shaken it off again.

In principle since Hiroshima and Nagasaki, in fact since the early Sixties, the problem of war and peace has radically changed. I made these considerations the central point of a lecture I gave in Peking, where, under a previous leadership, there had been support for the thesis of the inevitability of another great war. By now, even in the Middle Kingdom, opinion had swung round to an understanding that prevention of war was in their own and the general interest.

But what about limited wars waged for national and social freedom? What about defence against hostile interference in a country's own affairs? What about protection from aggressors? Can one leave a small and threatened state unprotected? Should it be left to the East to provide material equipment for liberation movements in southern Africa? Does not the shortage of food and medicine create a kind of war situation of its own? At this juncture I cannot help pointing out that violent conflicts of a new and more comprehensive nature become more and more probable if we turn our backs on the hungry regions. And the battle against hunger can be won only on earth.

The struggle against the arms race, against the danger of a Third World War which would annihilate everything (or almost everything), together with the struggle against world hunger and underdevelopment remains the top priority. However, the struggle for freedom and equality of nations is not a contradiction to that.

Democracy is not secured by the use of secret agents to carry out secret operations in defiance of international law. Freedom is not won with bombs, executions or other forms of terrorism. But who would condemn someone else for taking a social-militant path when the peaceful way is barred?

When global war is ruled out because it would mean the end,

the struggle of any movement, whatever it may be, has its limits where responsibility to humanity and humanitarian considerations begin. However, the dangers to mutual peace surely do not lie in the ardent striving for freedom of underprivileged peoples, nor even in the barely comprehensible irrationality of this or that region of the world, but in the tendency of third parties to meddle in the affairs of others or export the East–West conflict. A global peace policy and obligations capable of being monitored, are called for to counteract that.

Nationalistic and hegemonistic reasons, and moral convictions too, may sometimes urge one to go to the aid of the oppressed, by the most drastic of means if need be. And yet experience and insight tell us to bring judicious restraint to bear on our humanitarian and idealistic impulses, putting them into practice with reason as well as passion. In this context it should be obvious that the responsibility of every state grows with the weight of its power.

In the autumn of 1973, I respectfully reminded the United Nations of Gandhi's policy of non-violent resistance. I think now, as I did then, that an additional comment is called for. There is such a thing as violence exercised through toleration, intimidation through inactivity, threats through passivity, manslaughter committed by a failure to act. That is a border at which we should not stop – 'for it can mean the border between survival and extinction'.

9. Human Rights Are for All

The right to life is the most basic of all human rights, and those who fail to keep men, women and children from starving to death transgress against it for a start. This is the first thing to be mentioned when we speak of human rights. What do freedom, justice and dignity mean to those who go hungry to bed today, not knowing if they will eat tomorrow? In other words: social and liberal human rights go together.

Human rights are trampled upon in many countries of the world. What, then, can we do to keep more and more people from recurrent dreadful suffering? Ought terrorism to rule out development aid? Could the subject not to be put more forcefully to the United Nations? And could not at least the Europeans agree on a common position?

These questions are understandable. But one may indeed doubt, and not just with reference to developing countries, whether one punishes rulers by striking at their victims. In any case, we should not adopt too righteous an attitude, forgetting what European history looks like, or the fact that German criminals brought torment, bloodshed and death down on humanity little more than a generation ago. Even today, it would be an inadmissible simplification to make human rights a stick with which to beat only those states whose governments are not democratic, or to permit any impression that a reference to 'human rights' really means 'American rights'.

The extent to which torture is practised in Third World countries cannot but horrify us. Amnesty International's 1984 report names many countries: 27 African, 16 Asian and 15 Latin-American states have made systematic use of cruel and degrading treatment to oppress political dissidents or to suppress, if not actually to annihilate, ethnic and religious minorities.

No constitution, no statute book, no code of criminal procedure describes torture as a reliable method of getting 'information', or allows it as a means of execution. And yet torture is to some extent methodically developed and to some extent systematically employed. There are indications from Latin America that torture is taught and disseminated there in supra-national establishments; we may doubt whether the experts who teach it are exclusively South American.

Let it be remembered, lest we overlook the mote in our own eye, that torture is by no means unknown in our latitudes. It was more widespread in Europe in the sixteenth and seventeenth centuries, when methods and degrees of torture were highly developed. Only in the wake of the Enlightenment was torture abolished – officially, at any rate – as a judicial measure and, with the advent of progressive constitutional and liberal thought, discredited as an affront to human dignity. Today the prohibition of any kind of 'torture or cruel, inhuman or degrading treatment

The global balance-sheet of death is depressing:

- Over half a million and probably more than a million of the Khmer people of Kampuchea have died.
- And what about the massacres perpetrated by Emperor Bokassa, not really such a comical figure? Or Idi Amin's 'Lumpen-militariat'? 300,000 or more died, many of them after being tortured, out of a population of 12 million, and even five years later there was no end to the violence.
- How are we to understand the excesses committed in the name of the Prophet? Or the terror in the Middle East? Or the sufferings exacted from the Afghans?
- According to reports from Amnesty International, over a million people have been murdered by order of governments, or with governmental collusion, over the last ten years. The horrors that occur are often the systematic work of a state-controlled machine, the victims are men and women from all classes of society. Children are tortured in Central America. Children have been forced to watch their mothers tortured in the Middle East.
- The bloody conflicts in Sri Lanka, most conspicuous among them being the terror inflicted on the Tamil minority, have aroused indignation, and not only in India.
- The plight of the Kurds, denied a peaceful existence and a secure future by several of the states to which they are indigenous, can only inspire helpless despair.
- In 1984 Amnesty International, looking back over the previous year, stated that political prisoners had been killed, or tortured, or subjected to degrading treatment, in at least 117 of the over 150 sovereign states of the world. That was stated also with reference to China, Indonesia and Pakistan. Amnesty particularly criticized the Soviet Union for consigning dissidents to psychiatric hospitals.

or punishment' (the wording used in Article 6 of the Universal Declaration of Human Rights of 10 December 1948) is part of our understanding of human rights.

A retreat into autocratic or dictatorial forms of government has generally brought torture in its wake. In my speech accepting the

Nobel Prize I said: 'We have learned into what barbarism humanity can relapse. No religion, no ideology, no brilliant display of culture can exclude beyond all doubt the possibility that hatred may erupt from the depths of the human spirit and drag nations down into the depths.'

Torture was also a phenomenon accompanying colonialism; the final phase of French rule in Algeria attained a sad notoriety. It may thus be that the use of torture in the Third World is also a colonial legacy, just as political acts of violence in general are a prime article of export. Today an African professor need fear no contradiction when he says that, in his own part of the world, the technology of destruction is far in advance of productive techniques.

The deliberations of the 1975 convention which ended in unanimous condemnation of torture and other cruel, inhuman or degrading treatment or punishment seem to be making headway, but with what practical significance? The expedient of international ostracism is to the fore, and should really apply to international aid in the context of torture too. In future the prohibition of torture ought also to apply to exceptional situations such as those involving martial law or the threat of war. And an order from a superior should not be accepted as justification. For the rest, one should beware of the illusion that corrupt civilians are any better or more harmless than corrupt members of the armed forces. The mere existence of a written constitution is no guarantee of constitutionality. And the application of Western European criteria to the whole world is misleading anyway. So far as Africa is concerned, tribal realities currently carry more weight than the prospect of a multi-party system.

And what do the criteria of human rights signify in view of vast refugee movements? In the summer of 1984, the United Nations High Commissioner for Refugees, my former Danish colleague Paul Hartling, spoke of four million refugees in Africa alone. In fact, there are more refugees today than ever before in human history; for some years, two to three thousand people have joined their ranks daily.

• In this century, 250 million people have so far fled from their homes.

- According to Hartling's information, the number of new refugees has remained constant at 10 million over the last five years.
- Pakistan alone estimated the number of predominantly Afghan refugees there at about 2.5 million; there are probably more than 1.5 million in Iran.

It is as true today as it ever was that the international community of states in general, and democracies in particular, must take the victims of intolerance and brutality under their wing. Countries next door to any regime that causes an exodus of refugees have a great burden to bear. It should be shared, in a spirit of solidarity, by the better off. The Federal Republic of Germany cannot avoid realizing this basic insight. The fact that we cannot be a haven for all the tormented and outcast of the world, certainly not for all who would just like to be better off, is another matter – but that is not the real point at issue.

We must also face the challenge presented by the victims of South African apartheid. If even conservative circles in the United States say that 'peaceful change' is in their own interests, then more Europeans than before must try to work towards that change. Black South Africans not only have to bear the humiliating burden of apartheid; many of them are condemned to live below the poverty line in the 'homelands'.

The European Community has tried, without much success, to add a clause on human rights to the new Lomé Convention. It will continue to be sensible not to make development aid dependent on clauses demanding 'good conduct'. To determine what constitutes good conduct in a given case is a difficult undertaking anyway. In addition, there is by no means always a clear connection between human needs and the conduct of governments. It is a most debatable point whether aid for the poor helps to stabilize dictatorial régimes. In any case, there is no evidence that the denial of aid in itself helps to shorten the life of such dictatorial régimes. The contrary seems to be the case.

Human solidarity cannot be limited by the bounds of diverse political systems. It carries conviction only if it takes universal effect. We must neither be blind in the left eye nor reel with shock when the Left represents democratic values. And those things denied to the majority of humanity contribute to the conflicts which impede the relations between states and threaten peace.

Not our own generation alone, but those of our children and our grandchildren are still prone to an unfortunate colonializing romanticism, which seen in the sober light of day is nothing but a far from romantic history of extermination. Yes, we have always entertained an idea of the noble savage, and the impressive dignity of children of nature. None the less, those children of nature were regarded as simple souls, and as a general rule might was right. How long ago was the perfidy of the conquistadores, the endless chain of broken promises and treaties, that turned free peoples into an endangered and isolated minority, and not in South America alone?

But more and more people are coming to realize that the pressure of problems which originally hung together, and are now once again interconnected in their effects, can be countered neither by the misty twilight of myths and legends nor by the alarming simplification of the past. Today, the appeal to reason and humanitarianism points the way to our own future.

So let us break through all callous attitudes to those who are endangered or actually threatened with extinction. We must keep our minds alert to all the misery that still, and unceasingly, arises from blind striving for power and the unscrupulous representation of particular interests.

And experience shows that development policies can further the process of democratization. There are many who should ensure that they are better informed, so that they will not be taken in by empty phrases; many must be active themselves, and make sure that what is done in their names or at their instigation has real meaning – in their own communities, churches, parties, in their schools and their unions and associations. And we ought to begin with ourselves.

INSTEAD OF AN AFTERWORD:
PEACE AND DEVELOPMENT

On 25 April 1985, I received the Third World Prize at the United Nations headquarters in New York. I made a speech of thanks which expressed the ideas and the content of this book, and my doubts of whether any real improvement is taking place. This was its text:

Let me begin with a confession. It crossed my mind that it might have made more sense not to deliver a lecture on this occasion today. That way one would have demonstrated that with all our speeches so far we have made little impact in averting those dangers that threaten the very existence of mankind.

But no one need fear, or hope, that I will not make a speech; otherwise I would not be here today.

In any case I would have wanted to express my deep-felt gratitude towards those who have bestowed this great honour upon me. In doing so I think of all those with whom I have had the pleasure of cooperating in recent years. Without an exchange of views and ideas, and without the encouragement of others, I would not have dared to step into that field strewn with pitfalls – that area that links peace and development.

Now it could rightly be said that there is really no need for another analysis of the state of the world; of its growing problems; of its immense dangers; of our persisting inability to change things for the better. Conclusions have been drawn from the many analyses made – in terms of methods, substance and policies, even in terms of institutions. There is a wealth of proposals and formulas, in almost all areas. They range from economics to armaments; from currency and finance to hunger;

from drought and deforestation to the rapid growth of world population. There is a wide choice for everyone willing to choose. The supermarket of world problems and their solutions offers a complete inventory. There is hardly any gap on the shelves.

However, demand is not very strong. And this is so despite the fact that the vast majority of those who bear political responsibility for their people and nations are full of good will, and intend to solve the problems and let our world reach a state of security and well-being: a state which in accordance with the abilities of its members, could overcome oppressive misery and develop its immense resources.

I do not want to play anything down nor to paper it over. Of course there are those unable to do anything even if they wanted to. And there are those who take it upon themselves to do what they should not: the authors and victims of ideological presumptions, including the nice but ineffective preachers of a world without violence. Let us be quite clear: when I speak of peace I am thinking of all those who suffer from war or who are oppressed by it. But what concerns me today is worldwide rearmament and the obvious dangers of war, and their objective stark contrast to meaningful development, national and international.

To put it more forcibly: There is no point in worrying about cooperation and mutual interests, if we fail to avoid a nuclear holocaust; or if we fail to master the consequences of famine on continental scales.

People of my age have more than once known the experience of war leading to hunger. Can one deny today that hunger and mass misery can create the conditions from which new wars arise?

Indeed, alarming contradictions are a sign of our times. Our objective ability to solve most problems has grown almost as much as our capacity to destroy everything. Science and technology have made mankind capable of both, to a previously unimagined degree. Scientific and technical discoveries grow at seemingly unlimited speed. We are becoming aware of new dangers and new problems. But it seems as if mankind is helpless in the face of the irrepressible flood of new discoveries – yet unable to master the opportunities they offer.

Here one cannot but remember the genius of Albert Einstein who – like other great minds – had the gift of reducing highly complex processes to a simple formula. I am referring to his statement that the atomic bomb has changed everything except the mind and thinking of people. Indeed, he who looks for reasons why what should and could be done doesn't happen will find that *homo sapiens* has developed the technical, and in a narrower sense the economic, capabilities of his brain much faster than his political and community-building abilities. Or one might say that the formation of character and of moral values has not kept pace with the rapid progress of technology. Those are the qualities needed to live with oneself and to deal with oneself, and with others, with one's neighbours – on both a personal as much as a national plane. The economy aims for output and profit, today no less than 2,000 years ago. Weapons are geared towards easier handling, greater distance and precision just as for the past 2,000 years. And the conflicts between people and nations: the criteria by which we measure them – sovereignty, prestige, power, dominance, hatred towards the enemy – unfortunately all this has changed little in 2,000 years.

There is one exception: it is slowly dawning that we cannot go on behaving as we used to some hundred or even fifty years ago if we all want to survive.

The fear that human history may end could give grounds for hope. But fear, as a general rule, is not a reliable prop. Where then are we to find the strength to change our way of thinking, and what shall our criteria be?

Historically, there have been three basic attitudes in the relations between peoples and states: conflict, co-existence, cooperation. Nobody can argue that is no longer the case today. In conflicts between villages, tribes and nations many lives have been lost. But mankind could afford it. Even today, as long as these conflicts are local or regional, as long as they are sufficiently limited, we continue that way. A global conflict, however, would mean the end for all of us: a nuclear winter would descend even on those who now live in perpetual summer.

If survival is the top priority – and I can think of nothing else on which we could more easily agree among religions, ideologies and scientific viewpoints – then the preservation of world peace is our most important objective, dominating all others. Only if we avoid the self-destructive catastrophe of mankind will we be able to continue quarrelling about our different ideas, about the best way to achieve happiness for all. An end to global conflict without compromise is the precondition for coexistence and cooperation. Or put another way: without it a continuation of history appears impossible.

In global terms this means that worldwide there is no alternative to common security. The report of the Independent Commission on Disarmament and Security Issues under the chairmanship of Olof Palme, the Swedish Prime Minister, elaborated on necessary details three years ago.

The world can afford the coexistence of peoples and nations with their different views, the multiplicity of their ideas – real or imagined – on paths to welfare or happiness. Peoples and states may even turn their backs on each other as long as they do not dispute each other's right to exist. This holds worldwide; but it would also apply regionally, as the world might still be able to countenance regionally limited conflicts – terrible as they may be. The Gulf War, by the way, is a frightening example of how a military conflict of this kind can start with arms supplied by both superpowers which then find it difficult to control or stop what is happening.

Some of those wielding a great deal of power may admit it or not: by and large our actual interdependencies are increasing and the objective need for cooperation is growing. The debt crisis is a threat not only to the nations of Latin America; extremely high interest rates in the United States create problems for many other countries, not the least for the weakest among them. Drought and large-scale starvation in Africa do not stop at national borders. The energy crisis – which is far from over and which is not just an oil crisis; the threat of a drinking water crisis; the various ecological threats which had been largely neglected for a long time – all these problems extend across borders between political systems. I am sure the World Commission on Environment and Development chaired by Mrs Gro Harlem Brundtland will provide the international community with important additional suggestions in this area. My own country, the Federal Republic of Germany, suffers from acid rain and dying forests no less than its neighbours, the German Democratic Republic, Czechoslovakia or Switzerland.

In sum, many of our problems are of a global nature, they transcend systems, and their number is growing. Reason calls for the adoption of global rules far beyond the traditional ones, and it calls for mechanisms which guarantee the observation of such rules. It seems of little importance whether or not this is called a matter of mutual interest.

Egoism and narrow-mindedness have so far prevented any rapid progress in areas where the East–West conflict and North–South issues interact – in fact developments have advanced at a snail's pace at best. And it shows a considerable degree of stubbornness if people still refuse to admit that immensely rising worldwide military expenditure is not only politically damaging but does a lot of harm economically.

Those US$1,000 billion which the world spends on military purposes this year really amount to a death sentence for millions of human beings. The resources which they would need for living are actually spent on armaments.

But there is another obstacle to understanding the need to see ourselves more as partners in common security, in military and in economic terms; there is not only stubbornness but also the lust for power. Nobody can deny that the desire for power in individuals as in nations is a strong motivation which, when it comes to most mistakes and catastrophes in the development of mankind, we cannot explain away. One could even see our history as a development in which force – in its unrestricted expression, also known as the law of the jungle – had to give way step by step to the rule of law, although there were many setbacks. Limits and rules of behaviour were adopted which everyone has to observe. Each treaty voluntarily agreed is another step in this direction.

Celebrating their fortieth anniversary this year, the United Nations stand as a symbol of a step forward – and of the inevitable difficulties associated with it. The mechanism of the Security Council and the veto may be taken as evidence of the cool realism of its founders who knew that it would have been too much to expect a world organization to overcome real power by schematic majority rule. One might also say: joint decisions, agreed rules and comprehensive arrangements within the United Nations as well as elsewhere demand the cooperation of the powerful, especially of the superpowers.

Here we have witnessed a development since 1945 which in the context with which I am concerned nobody has expressed better than President Raúl Alfonsín of Argentina. As you know he belongs to the group of six heads of state and government from five continents who got together last year to voice their own and many other people's concern and their alarmed impatience with regard to arms control. In January at their meeting in New Delhi the President of Argentina stressed the legitimate interests of big powers and superpowers, in particular regarding their security from each other and thus their ability to defend themselves. But, he made it clear, it is an undeniable fact that their military forces and their weapons' arsenals have grown far beyond their defensive requirements. They have acquired the capability – only the two superpowers have it and nobody else – to eradicate all life from this planet. Thus their power has objectively become a threat to all people. The decision to use those weapons is exclusively theirs. This implies that some individuals, their advisors, small élites – few people in any case – hold the power to destroy the basic right of all people; their right to live.

In all civilizations and cultures, in all religions of all societies and continents, the right to live was considered something special. Therefore, it is unacceptable to the 5 billion people or to the 160 states, it is terrifying, that they should depend in their right to live on a small group of people in one or two capitals; that they should have to trust in the wisdom and restraint of those few not to abuse their power and not to make that one irreversible mistake. The preservation of world peace is too fundamental a human right, and a right of nations, to be left to the leadership of superpowers alone.

From that right to live all those of us with less power derive our right to put pressure on the two superpowers to limit their power and to agree on common rules of conduct in the interest of maintaining world peace. This would not reduce their power. And I entertain no thoughts of neglecting political differences. But a global code for preserving world peace must be effective especially for those very powers who hold the means to destroy it.

When the President of the United States and the leader of the Soviet Union meet in the near future – here in New York or elsewhere – the world does not necessarily expect them to become

friends, or to wipe away their differences by magic. They are not
expected to announce cooperation in matters where there can be
no consensus. We do expect them, however, to end the threat of
an all-destructive world conflict. Obviously this will only be
possible if they do not question each other's right to exist. And
only if they manage to agree that they themselves will only be able
to achieve security together – and thus banish the danger of
extinction which threatens all of us.

This would mean at least an interruption of the arms race while
negotiations continue. And it means negotiations on critical areas
as much as on destabilizing military projects. It also means
confronting the links between the arms race and development,
between hunger and weapons, and making this issue part of the
agenda.

To me the aim of such an urgently needed summit meeting of
the superpowers should be nothing short of an agreement which
rules out a Third World War. This would mean more than most
of what is being said now as we look back to May and August of
1945. It would mean nothing less than the opening of a new
chapter in the history of mankind.

Peoples and states must demand such an agreement, otherwise
security is not to be found – either in East–West problems which
will continue to exist, or in North–South problems which become
ever more pressing. On the basis of such an agreement many
issues would be easier to control, and the export of East–West
controversies into the Third World could probably be reduced. A
halt to further excessive arms build-ups would become plausible.
And the ever-increasing accumulation of destructive machinery
would come to be seen as even more perverse – an arsenal which
kills people without ever being used because it eats up the money
without which people are condemned to death through starvation.

When the United Nations hold their Special Conference on
disarmament and development in 1986 – once more drawing on
the commendable work of the group of experts chaired by Inga
Thorsson – much will depend on curbing the tendency to trot out
tedious propaganda slogans on the one hand and to discuss
abstract anaemic theories on the other. Nor must participants be
held back by the self-declared realists who accompany their

inaction with nicely chosen rhetoric about disarmament and development being objectives too important each in its own right to be linked together. Even if only modest amounts would be affected in the beginning, the redirection of resources should be made a reality and as soon as possible. And this should include a discussion of the rather dubious and damaging aspects of much of what constitutes the international arms market.

However, it is only on the basis of an agreement which rules out a Third World War that we will be able to choose easily or indeed at all between the proposals for resolving the North–South conflict. This will become immediately obvious when we think of the forthcoming Geneva talks. How can one ever decide on what steps to take without first having made the new perspectives clear?

Now, as for North–South issues, it will come as no surprise to you if I reiterate the proposals – which ranged from emergency measures to structural reforms – presented by the Independent Commission which I chaired. Most of our findings remain valid today. It would have been better if we could actually claim that some problems had been resolved positively. Unfortunately this is predominantly not the case, and many issues today present themselves in yet more serious terms.

Many of those points surfaced again when representatives of non-aligned countries put their suggestions for a realistically comprehensive dialogue down on paper. And also when Indira Gandhi, who will live on in our memory, envisaged another North–South summit for the second half of 1985. But instead, we now witness considerable skills being applied in the areas of currency and finance to patch up holes, but the necessary reforms being avoided. The same goes for international trade and other areas well known to all of us.

As yet we see no sign of action which might set in motion what has ground to a standstill in such a frustrating way: I mean the intended 'global' discussion, under the auspices of the United Nations, about those issues important to a restructuring of worldwide economic relations. The responsibility for the complete failure has to be lain at several doors. But one thing is clear: if certain important countries had been willing to move, a general deadlock would not have come to pass.

I stress the paramount responsibility of the superpowers. At the same time I want to warn the big countries – and all others concerned – not to allow the destruction of multilateralism and its institutions, imperfect as they may be. Europe should, and must, realize that it has to play a role in counteracting negative developments. There is no reason why Europe should always wait for others to take the lead. And much less should it jump on band-wagons which may be big but are moving in the wrong direction – or ending up nowhere.

When I speak of multilateralism, I want to emphasize that there is still more scope for it in a peace-keeping role, than many people believe. The decisions which the superpowers must inevitably make would harmonize well with better use of the peace-keeping potential of the United Nations. And a fresh, serious look should be taken at the conciliatary powers of both the Security Council and the Secretary-General.

At the same time it is of primary importance that the rest of us who have power neither over the bomb nor the veto, are no longer allowed to lose sight of the links between crises of security, world economy and environment. I would like to use the award be-stowed upon me as a contribution towards an independent clearing house for 'Peace and Development' which would bring together realistic ideas from all over the world, and thus establish a constructive link between East–West and North–South issues.

I am now coming close again to making proposals whose practical value I questioned at the beginning of my lecture. Presumably it has become clear where, in my view, the key to a solution of our most pressing problems lies. Disputes will lead nowhere as long as they are about isolated issues, such as debts or commodities, food or birth-rates, or soil erosion, deforestation and other appalling environmental damage. Or on whether attribution of blame and responsibilities should be on a national or international level. On budgets too, and absurdities of budgets which allocate funds for armaments that are lacking for educa-tion or health care. The key to a solution not of all but of many problems is in the hands of the superpowers. The question is whether they can succeed in limiting their fruitless conflict and their power to destroy the world, at least to the extent of agreeing on a code which would make a Third World War impossible.

That cannot mean that the rest of us should hide behind the responsibility of the nuclear giants. We must shoulder our own responsibilities. And this includes applying all possible pressure and telling the powerful of this world what they owe mankind.

I put it this way: since there can be no survival without the prevention of a Third World War, since development means peace, we must at last begin to organize ourselves to cooperate and give peaceful development a chance. That chance is in trust for all of us and alone gives us hope that future generations will actually live after us.